ENVIRONMENT AND SOCIAL CONCERNS

About the Editors

Dr. Venu Trivedi, Prof. and Head, Department of Geography, Govt. Post Graduate Girls College, Motitabela, Indore, former Chairperson, Board of Studies, Geography, Devi Ahilya Vishwavidyalaya, Indore, Member, Central Board of Studies, M.P., Member, Board of Studies, Sarojini Naidu, Post Graduate Girls' College, Bhopal and Research Guide in Geography Devi Ahilya Vishwavidyalaya, Indore, M.P. published 22 research papers in established geographical journals. She has successfully completed Minor Research Project of University Grants Commission, Bhopal in 2008 and organised a National Conference on "Environmental Problems and Initiatives" in 2007.

Prof. V.K. Shrivastava, educated at Jabalpur, Sagar and London, is the former Head of Department of Geography, Deen Dayal Upadhyaya Gorakhpur University, Gorakhpur where he served from 1963 to 1999. He was the Chairman of International Geographical Union Commission for four years. He spent about five years at Dr. H.S. Gour University, Sagar, as Visiting Professor and Emeritus fellow. He has produced five research monographs, edited half a dozen research volumes and written a dozen text books in Geography. Presently, he is executing a research project sponsored by Indian Council of Social Science Research, New Delhi, in the Department of Geography of Rani Durgawati Vishwavidhyalaya, Jabalpur.

Environment
and
Social Concerns

Edited by

Venu Trivedi
V.K. Shrivastava

CONCEPT PUBLISHING COMPANY PVT. LTD.
NEW DELHI-110 059

ISBN-13: 978-81-8069-751-7

First Published 2011

Published and Printed by

Concept Publishing Company Pvt. Ltd.
Regd. Office:
A/15-16, Commercial Block, Mohan Garden
New Delhi-110059 (India)
Phones : 25351460, 25351794, *Fax* : 091-11-25357109
Email : publishing@conceptpub.com,
Website: www.conceptpub.com

Editorial Office:
H-13, Bali Nagar, New Delhi-110 015, India.

Cataloging in Publication Data--*Courtesy:* D.K. Agencies (P) Ltd. <docinfo@dkagencies.com>

Environment and social concerns / edited by Venu Trivedi, V.K. Shrivastava.
p. cm.
Includes bibliographical references and index.
ISBN 9788180697517

1. Pollution--Social aspects--Congresses. 2. Pollution--Social aspects--India--Indore--Congresses. 3. Pollution--Social aspects--India--Madhya Pradesh--Congresses. 4. Environmental sociology--Congresses. 5. Environmental degradation--Congresses. 6. Environmental management--Congresses. I. Trivedi, Venu. II. Shrivastava, V. K. (Virendra Kumar), 1939-

DDC 304.209543 22

Dedicated to
Late Prof. Vijaya Phanse

Prof. A.A. Abbasi

I.D.A. Plot No. 80 E.B.
Scheme No. 94,
INDORE (M.P.)
Phone No.: 0731-4041595

Foreword

The concern which the enlightened people have been showing towards environmental degradation all over the world during the past five decades is not only academic rather it is the concern of the entire humanity about its very existence. The Rio, Stockholm, Tokyo and Copenhagen Conferences were held in the same context. The discussions revolved around the growing imbalance among the various components of natural environmental culminating in the present scenario of the degrading environment.

Geographers have always studied the deep yet delicate relationship between physical and biospheres. They have provided solid and practical solutions to cope with the problems of environmental systems.

I am happy that Dr. Venu Trivedi has very carefully edited the research papers submitted in the conference in order to

Former Vice Chancellor, Indore University (DAVV) Indore (M.P.)
Retired Professor of Geography
Member, University Grants Commission (Scove), New Delhi
Member, Human Rights Commission, Ayog Mitra, Indore
Member, M.P. State Urdu Academy, Bhopal
Member, National Integration Committee, M.P., Bhopal
Member, Executive Council, Vikram University, Ujjain
Member, Governing Body, Baba Saheb Ambedkar Institute, Mhow
General Secretary, Centre for Environment Protection Research and Development, Indore
Hony. Director, Kund Kund Gyanpeeth, Indore

present a holistic picture of the various environmental factors. It is also very thoughtful that the volume has been dedicated to a popular and able professor of Geography late Dr. Vijay Phanse.

Prof. A.A. Abbasi

Preface

The book titled 'Environment and Social Concern' reflects the anxiety of a young geographer that the contributions made by an assembly of scientists focusing discussions on a theme ought to be broughtout in a book form before they are put out of ones mind. This apprehension swayed over the mind of the young geographer who convened the conference. The result is the book in hand and the young geographer is Dr. Venu Trivedi. This modest attempt has it in mind that there is no better gift to society than to make it known that the academic faculty is deeply concerned with the alarming danger to quality of life. It also displays that the imprints of events like the one which this book mirrors ought to be preserved and the contributions that such events may have got to be added to the contemporary field of knowledge.

Reminiscences of a former colleague, like late Prof. Vijaya Phanse, which the land of Malwa has offered, on such an occasion underlines the concern that the courage and conviction so rightly demonstrated by our predecessor still inspires us. Prof. Vijaya Phanse was a teacher passionately involved with colleagues and students in teaching and research at Government Arts and Commerce College of Indore. With the short span of life that God granted to her she could inspire a generation. Her vibrant years have left an imprint that good teaching and able administration are constructive tools for providing positive feedback to society from academic institutions. The gap left by her still remains to be fulfilled and in this sense the dedication of the proceedings of the National Seminar in her fond memory is a complimentary gesture.

The volume in hand has been divided into five sections. Environmental concerns and consequent social responses have been underlined in context of social justice, sustainability, impact of retailing on environment, role of floriculture in improving the quality of environment and involving women actively in protecting the environment. Dimensions of environmental problems related to pollution of land, air and water have been richly discussed and demonstrated in the second section of the book which encompasses human activities from agriculture to nuclear pollution. The beauty of the book lies in the integrated presentation of papers related from pure and physical sciences to humanities. The third section of the book demonstrate that human creativity can make an attempt to compensate the loss to environment by creating wealth from waste, by planning and management of environment. The fourth section demonstrates a concern for the depleting quality of urban life by taking examples from the city of Indore. The social concerns call attention to study the state of environment, examine the dimensions of environmental problems and to present a collaborative model for environmental planning and management. The book in hand has specified a right and proper awareness in perceiving the state of environment of the city of Indore, the venue of the National Conference 'Environmental Problems and Initiatives'. The public image of the event which this book embodies is preserved in the last section.

The conference was a great success by the participation of academicians from younger age group in a large number. They even demonstrated their concern for environment and society through poster sessions and through assessment of concurrent river projects undertaken in the State of Madhya Pradesh and their impact on society and environmental quality in general. The interdisciplinary nature of the event was a rare phenomenon where experts from pure and applied sciences also joined in enriching the contents of the conference.

V.K. Shrivastava
Emeritus Fellow
Department of Geography
Rani Durgawati Vishwavidyalaya
Jabalpur, M.P.

Acknowledgements

With a deep sense of gratitude I wish to acknowledge the help, assistance and advise of all those who have joined me in making the National Conference a success. The generous financial assistance of the University Grants Commission, New Delhi, is acknowledged with a sense of obligation. They have carried a tradition of providing financial assistance to colleges for organizing academic events and without this assistance the event might not have been organized. The patronage offered by Prof. A.A. Abbasi goes a long way in charting the course of academic events in our field. I have no words to thank him for his generosity in encouraging his students like me. We also acknowledge with thanks the guidance and help provided by Additional Director, Dr. N.K. Dad. I would be failing in my duties if I do not acknowledge the help provided by Prof. V.K. Shrivastava and Prof. Y.G. Joshi in organizing this event.

Friends, my College administration so graciously assisted us in every aspect of the organization. Our Principal, Dr. Manjula Choubey, and the entire administrative staff deserves our heartfelt thanks for their cooperation. I am equally grateful to my colleagues in the Department of Geography who ceaselessly worked round the clock in making the event a success. They have helped me in every aspect of the conference. The students of the Department of Geography also joined us wholeheartedly in this conference. I can never forget the inspiration I received from Shri K.L. Trivedi, my father and Dr. Harsh Vyas, my husband.

Lastly, but not the least, the concern for focusing on geography shown by Concept Publishing Company, Pvt. Ltd., New Delhi, also deserves mention. But for their graceful approach in the publishing world this book might not have been brought in the shape in which it rests in our hands. Concept Publishing Company Pvt. Ltd. bears the spirit of Geography and one must thank Mr. Ashok Kumar Mittal for amiably undertaking the work.

Indore

Venu Trivedi
Convenor

Contents

SECTION C: TECHNO-POLITICAL RESPONSES

SECTION D: FOCUS ON INDORE CITY AND ITS ENVIRONMENT

SECTION E: PUBLIC IMAGE

SECTION F: ABSTRACTS OF HINDI PAPERS PRESENTED IN THE SEMINAR AND RECOMENDATIONS

List of Contributors

Alka Neema, Assistant Professor, Department of Chemistry, Government Girls P.G. College, Motitabela, Indore (M.P.).

Anamika Jain, Professor, Department of Chemistry, Government Girls P.G. College, Motitabela, Indore (M.P.).

Anjula Poius, Assistant Professor, New Science College, Indore (M.P.).

Archana Kanthed, Assistant Professor, Government Girls P.G. College, Motitabela, Indore (M.P.).

Bhakti Chourey, Assistant Professor, Department of Geography, Government Girls P.G. College, Motitabela, Indore (M.P.).

Bhatt, S., Department of Physics, Government N.S. Science College, Indore (M.P.).

Bhole, R.V., Department of Geography, Dr. A.G.D. Bendale Mahila Mahavidyalaya, Jalgaon (M.S.).

Bindu Gandhi, Assistant Professor, Government Girls P.G. College, Motitabela, Indore (M.P.).

Dhake, S.V., Department of Geography, Dr. A.G.D. Bendale Mahila Mahavidyalaya, Jalgaon (M.S.).

Dipanita Gargava, Assistant Professor, Department of English, Gujrati Girls Collge, Indore (M.P.).

Joshi, Y.G., Dean, Academics, Dr. Babasaheb Ambedkar National Institute of Social Sciences, Mhow (M.P.).

Jyoti Doodhiya, Assistant Professor, Department of Chemistry, Government Girls P.G. College, Motitabela, Indore (M.P.).

Kaur, D. Professor and Head, Department of Geography, Government Arts and Commerce College, Indore (M.P.).

Manisha Dandawate, B.P. Post Graduate College, Mhow (M.P.).

Naresh Kumar, Assistant Professor, Department of Geography, Government S.K.P. College, Dewas (M.P.).

Nilosey, V., Professor, Department of Chemistry, Government Girls P.G. College, Motitabela, Indore (M.P.).

Patil, V.J., Department of Geography, Dr. A.G.D. Bendala Mahila Mahavidyalaya, Jalgaon (M.S.).

Rajshri Somani, Assistant Professor, Department of Chemistry, Government Girls P.G. College, Motitabela, Indore (M.P.).

Rashmi Gupta, Professor, Department of Economics, Government P.G. College, Motitabela, Indore (M.P.).

Rekha Killedar, Professor and Head, Department of Chemistry, Government Girls P.G. College, Motitabela, Indore (M.P.).

Sadhna Saxena, Assistant Professor, Government Girls P.G. College, Motitabela, Indore (M.P.).

Sanjay Prabhune, Department of Chemistry, Government Girls P.G. College, Motitabela, Indore (M.P.).

Savita Kanwar, Government Girls P.G. College, Motitabela, Indore (M.P.).

Seema Tripathi, Government Madhav Science College, Ujjain (M.P.).

Shoba Sharma, Assistant Professor, Department of Botany, Government Girls P.G. College, Motitabela, Indore (M.P.).

Shrivastava, Kum Kum Rani, Director, Geo-Marketing Laboratory, Gorakhpur.

Shrivastava, V.K., Emeritus Fellow, Hon. Director, ICSSR Research Project, Jabalpur (M.P.).

Subhra Biswas, Research Scholar, Department of Geography, Government Arts and Commerce College, Indore (M.P.).

Sunita Phadnis, Assistant Professor, Department of Chemistry, Government Girls P.G. College, Motitabela, Indore (M.P.).

Vandana Mishra, Assistant Professor of English, Government Girls P.G. College, Motitabela, Indore (M.P.).

Venu Trivedi, Professor and Head, Department of Geography, Government Girls P.G. College, Motitabela, Indore (M.P.).

Introduction

Environmental Problems and Initiatives

During the last few years India has suffered so many natural calamities and man-made problems. Flood hazards in Maharashtra especially in Mumbai, earthquakes in Bhuj-Gujarat, tsunami's terror in Tamil Nadu, cyclone's effect in coastal Orissa, unexpected drought in North-Eastern States and global warming are natural problems. On the other hand, some of the anthropogenic problems like ever increasing population, social conflicts, damaging impact of construction of big dams, leakages of toxic wastes, pollution, etc., have adverse impact upon the environment which are faced by our countrymen. As a matter of fact the whole world is facing ever increasing environmental problems. Development of science and technology is a demand of the modern age but at the cost of environment it is always harmful.

In view of these problems, the focal theme of two days' conference was selected as, "Environmental Problems and Initiatives". These problems are emerging from rapid economic development and anthropogenic transformation of space, pressure of population, disparities in lifestyle of people, etc. No doubt, the economic development of a region is a natural demand of the present time, their harmful consequences on various natural spheres and human habitats have yet to receive due attention. Development without a concern for the environment can only be development for a short term. In the long term, it will become anti-development and it can go on only at the cost of enormous human sufferings, increasing poverty and oppression.

Bearing this in mind, the problem may be discussed in many ways. The first and foremost important need is to analyze the causes responsible for these environmental problems. Since a single cause is not responsible for this burning issue, researchers should pay their due attention towards various responsible causes.

These problems may further be classified as they affect the society and people. Environmental problems in a way are social problems. They begin with people as the cause and end with people as their victims. They are usually born of ignorance or apathy. It is the people who create a bad environment and a bad environment brings out the worst for people.

The problems may be studied at local and regional level, so that remedial action could be planned. Each region has its own characteristics and these characteristics show the regional nature of the problem. It depends upon the character of the individual region, how it may respond and refer to development.

Environmental problems always affect places and people. Its effects may be on the region itself or on the lifestyle of human-beings. Environmental problems generate social responses and initiatives are taken by the society, NGOs, or government, Ministry of Environment and Forest, Government of India and Department of Science and Technology of each State Government who are deeply engaged in the protection, preservation and conservation of environment. Several possible policies, programmes and their implementation strategies have been evolved from time to time by government organization and NGOs towards their effort for better environmental management.

The environmental problems of developing countries are not just the side effects of excessive industrialization; they also reflect the inadequacies and lopsidedness of development. Progress has become synonymous with an assault on nature. Edward Thomson, a British writer, once said to Mahatma Gandhi that wild life was fast disappearing. Gandhiji remarked that it was decreasing in the jungles, but it was increasing in the towns. We need to learn from the mistakes made by affluent countries in this respect and with measures of scientific and technological development, we can still improve our living environment, and provide food, water, sanitation and shelter to the starving, homeless millions of the third world. By making deserts green and even Rocky Mountains habitable by proper environmental management and by creating environmental awareness among people, we can choose an ecologically compatible path of development.

The recommendations shall be very useful in planning for future environmental research and development.

I am sure that the deliberations of our conference during three days will be fruitful. I have no doubt that it will make a significant contribution in extending the frontiers of knowledge and experience in the field of various environmental problems and initiatives.

Prof. Venu Trivedi
Convener

SECTION-A

SOCIAL CONCERNS

1

Environmental Concerns, Social Responses and Initiatives

Y.G. Joshi

Introduction

Man-Environment interaction, its resulting spatial pattern and consequences have been the main focus of geographical studies in general, and human geography, in particular. Besides, the ideographic and nomothetic approaches aimed at deeper understanding of the theoretical aspects, the pragmatic approaches which were adopted in social sciences in the modern period necessitated deeper understanding of the behavioural aspects on the one hand, and a closer association of all the branches of social sciences and applied physical sciences, on the other. Environmental studies is also one of such fields where a closer understanding of various disciplines is necessary. Being an integrated discipline geography and geographers can play a leading role for a better understanding of the environmental processes at work, consequences of human intervention, and also for steering these interventions towards a desired direction. The emphasis of the present conference is also not restricted to a discussion on various aspects of environmental problems, but also to analyze the role of the society and various action groups towards monitoring these problems both at local and regional levels.

The scope of the seminar is quite vast, however, looking to the time constraint, I shall like to restrict my lecture to the following aspects:

1. Why there should be an environmental concern?
2. Clash of interest between different hierarchies and priorities, and
3. Why it is required to energize the micro systems?

Why a Concern?

Man has to learn from his past experiences if he wants to avoid future miseries. The past experience of rapid growth, urbanization, industrialization, coupled with existing growth of population and consumption demand, has compelled us to be concerned with our obsession with infinite growth. There has to be a limit to growth because it is neither sustainable nor is desirable. Man has to learn to live in harmony with nature. Although the dogma of "Determinism" may be called as the idea of the past, the limits provided by nature can never be denied. Prof. Raza (1991) had rightly pointed out that nature indicates the direction of its optimal appropriation and lays down the existing limits of human freedom.

As is depicted in the Fig. 1.1, change and continuity which are the basic laws of nature, can only be sustained by a balanced existence.

During past few decades it has been realized that though environment and development are complementary to each other, the environmental problems are largely the side effects of the development activities in various sectors. Further, the environmental problems are so linked to political, cultural and economic systems that the matter needs to be addressed at micro-level of the society, involving people's participation in environment related development activities.

Lately there had been a paradigm shift from growth to development and from economic development to human development. The conventional model of development has been replaced (at least in principle) by a model of development

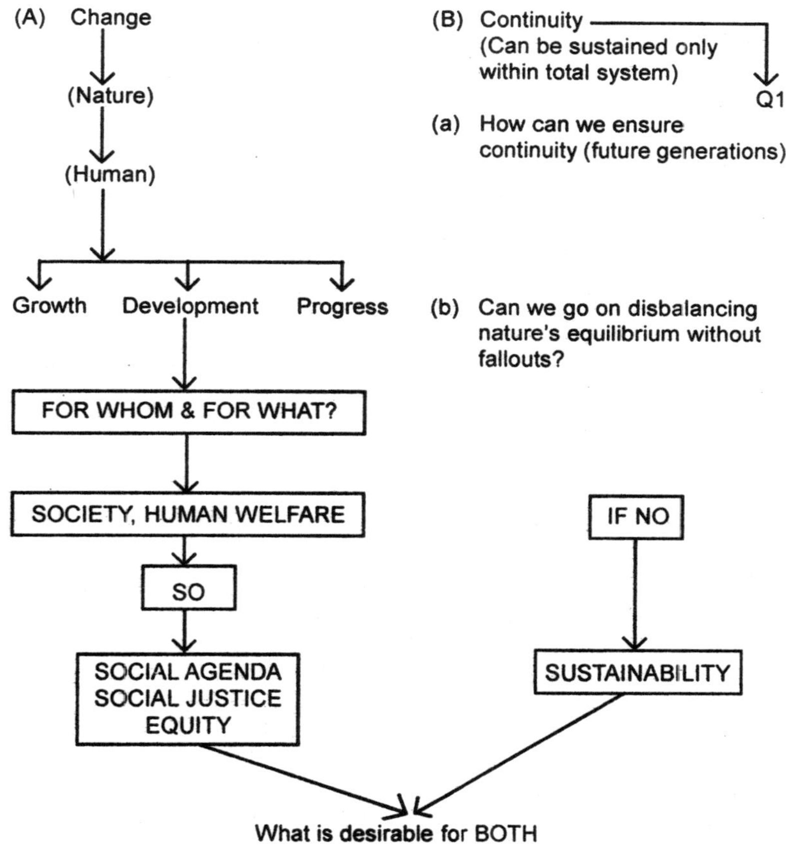

Fig. 1.1: Basic Laws of Nature

which is based on the principle of human dignity, equity and social justice. The emphasis is now on quality of development, as measured by (a) the participation of people in matters affecting their lives, (b) the nature of social and inter-personal relation, and (c) the relationship of people to their environment (Gangrade, 1995, 67).

The paradigm shift from economic development to "Sustainable Human Development" has been clearly defined in the UNDP Human Development Report, 1994. The new paradigm puts people at the centre of development, regards economic growth as a means and not the end, protects the life opportunities of future generations and respects the natural systems on which all the life depends. In this paradigm, development is conceived to be of the people, to be measured in terms of investment in human capital, for the people, i.e., ensuring a wider and fare distribution of the fruits of economic growth, and by the people, meaning that the opportunity to participate is provided to all.

Conceding the fact that the above mentioned paradigm shifts have compelled the policy-makers and planners at all levels (macro to micro) to shift their focus, it is also necesary to investigate whether this concern for environment remains only theoretical and cosmetic or is actually translated in practice. The ground realities show big gaps betwen theoreies and realities. The contemporary situation does not testify that our concern for environment has shifted from elite to poor, from developed areas to poor areas, and from GDP growth to eliminating poverty. The phenomenon increase of millionaires and corporate and mushrooming urban malls with a backdrop of a sizable population subsisting on Rs. 12 per day, thousands of farmers committing suicides and millions of poor people being uprooted from their traditional livelihood sources, very well testifies towards the fact that our concern is not real.

Thus, a strong message is to be given to the young generation that the theory-rich superficial concerns will not be sustainable for long and will have to be real, down to earth and participatory.

Clash of Interest between Different Hierarchies and Priorities

Much talked about global concern for bio-diversity, global warming, ozone depletion, etc., face stiff challenge towards implementation at regional and sub-regional levels. The main criticism of environment based global concern emerged during world summit at Rio-de-Jenaro (1992). A stiff resistance came from the activists of the developing nations against the imposition of global environmental views and legislations on the developing and poor countries.

The main objections were:

(a) The world view glosses over the question of regional disparity in the control and use of natural resources (north with one fifth population consumes 70 per cent energy, 75 per cent metal and 80 per cent wood (HDR, 1994).
(b) Inter-generational and inter-regional disparity. Right of the underdeveloped to grow and the responsibility of the north to compensate what they had been doing for last 200 years.
(c) Environment views should not be used by the north as a tool to curb development in the underdeveloped world.

The above mentioned contradictions expressed at global level also emerge during debates at national level where conflicts take place between regional and national concerns and between natural resource rich but economically poor areas and industry and service based rich urban regions. The increasing inter-state disputes for water, power and competing economic interests are corollary to the fact that our concern for environment has different connotations in different systems and sub-systems. Even the same political party changes its stand whenever regional interests override their national commitments. There is also differentiation between general environmental concerns and concerns in the environmentally stressed, sensitive and distressed areas.

Other than regional and sub-regional concerns, a challenge also emerges from within different economies and different groups, having different priorities. In India a large section of population, both in the rural and urban areas, live in sub-marginal condition where livelihood compulsions always override the concern for environment. As such, it is difficult to generalize the nature of concern. That is why the most modern theories are not in favour of generalizations. Pane Dubas, the late well known bacteriologist, coined the phrase "think globally, act locally" and opined that this was the way that an individual could help bring about a desirable future (quoted by Saitz, 1990, 70).

In short, it may be said that the environmental concerns should not be generalized to an extent that interests of different groups and areas, especially the marginal and sub-marginal ones, are ignored. Prof. Raza has rightly commented that national development is national only to the extent that it subsumes regional development, sustains it, and is sustained by it.

Why it is required to Energize the Micro-system

In Fig. 1.2, I have tried to show the interaction between different hierarchies of subsystems (Joshi, 1998, 124).

The diagram clarifies that due to low downward percolation from upper hierarchies and the incapability of a

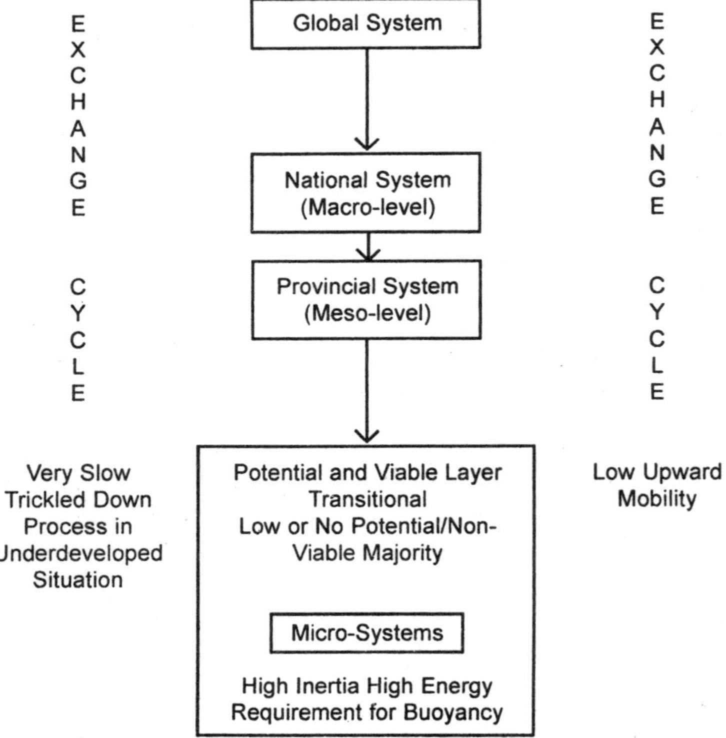

Fig. 1.2: Basic Laws of Nature

large section of society at a micro-level to compete and participate, the exchange cycle with the higher order system operates only with the upper creamy layer. This may be a reason of increased gap between the viable and non-viable classes. Thus, large-scale social response and initiative cannot be generated unless high inertia micro-systems are sufficiently energized to attain necessary buoyancy.

Lately, in the county there have been important ecological movements, viz., Chipko, Silent Valley, Bhopal tragedy, Narmada Bachao, etc., which were, though initiated by the middle class, could sufficiently mobilize large masses at the grass root level. The movements, not only generated mass environmental programmes, like large-scale aforestation in Arawali, water harvesting, watershed development and induction of the concept of social costing, but were also instrumental in the enactment of various environmental acts, like Public Viability Insurance Act, 1991, Hazardous Waste Rules, 1989 and Environmental Protection Act, 1986.

Looking to the importance of environmental movements there is a need to integrate and consolidate these micro-level efforts so that these are not reduced to cosmetic ones and remain restricted to local areas and are overpowered by vested interests and local politics. In this endeavour the young generation should have a major role to play and I am confident that they will actively participate in this programme of mass mobilization towards environmental concern.

REFERENCES

Gangrade, K.D. (1905), *Sorvoday Model of Development in Social Development and Justice in India*, R.G. Singh and R.D. Gadkar (eds.), New Delhi: Radient Publishers.

Human Development Report (1994), New York, Oxford University Press (Published for UNDP).

Joshi, Y.G. (1998), "A Quest for Social Justice in the Development Models" in Joshi and Verma (ed.) *Social Environment for Sustainable Development*, Rawat Publication, New Delhi.

Raza, Maris (1991), "Nature of Rural Urban Urban Interactions" *IASSI Quarterly*, Vol. X, No. 1, July–September, pp. 1-14.

Seitz, John L. (1988), *Politics of Development*, Bombay: Popular Prakashan.

2

Environmental Concerns and Retailing
The Case of Hats and Bazaars

V.K. SHRIVASTAVA

The paper focuses on the impact of retailing on environmental quality. Retailing is an activity with which the society in general is greatly concerned. Market places are the platforms for retailing. Normally the market place participants do not realize that retailing activities add to the pollution of environment. If this fact goes on unnoticed the environment which gets polluted at micro scale in day-to-day activities starts adding to pollution of land and air at larger scale. It is with this view in mind that the environmental concerns of retailing are being highlighted.

Socio-Econo-Cultural Components

Environmental concerns are mirrored in social responses and initiatives. *Hats* and *bazaars* are mirrors of spontaneous consequence of demand and supply equation of a society in relation to its environs. These socio-econo-cultural components of any region symbolize the end users of natural and human resources with a strong impulsive propensity of generating feed back mechanism that decides the prospects of development or de-generation of the society they serve. The prospects so created are reflected in the form of social harmony or conflicts on one hand and environmental degradation on the other. It is because environmental concerns represent social concerns.

Environmental Concerns vis-à-vis Social Concerns

The quality of environment is measured in its significance to man. Man is the end user of resources. Man consumes resources that cannot be re-generated. The magnitude of consumption, the mode of utilization of resources, the awareness about its impact on environment and the response of nature to activities of man are exhibited in the form of environmental problems which are the focus of discussion at present.

Bazaars and Environment

The *hats* and *bazaars* may be taken as icons of the symbiotic relationship between nature and man which also is the core of geography. An appraisal of the functioning of *hats* and *bazaars* which are common to rural and urban areas both may highlight their impact on problems of quality of environment and status of natural resources which becomes end product of man-environment interrelationship. It may be mentioned that the term 'retailing' has a complex structure in farming and non-farming (manufacturing) regions of the world. For the present study *hats* and *bazaars* represent a form of exchange of goods and services prevalent all over the world and they represent tertiary sector of the economy.

It may be said that marketing is a function as old as the history of inter-societal exchange relations of communities possessing or lacking typical resources. They are part and parcel of human ecosystem. The unmanageable and uncontrolled growth of any component of the ecosystem threatens its quality and endangers the balance among its components. It may then be said to be a source of pollution and may lead to de-generation of the natural and social fabric of a region. With this view in mind certain inherent attributes of market function may be taken as threat to environmental quality.

Functioning Of Bazaars

An appraisal of the functioning of *hats* and *bazaars* may highlight their impact on problems of quality of environment and status of natural resources which becomes end product of man-environment interrelationship.

Retailing: The Tertiary Sector

It may be mentioned that the term 'retailing' has a complex structure in farming and non-farming (manufacturing) regions of the world. For the present study *hats* and *bazaars* represent a form of exchange of goods and services prevalent all over the world and they represent tertiary sector of the economy.

Marketing: A Human Ecosystem

It may be said that marketing is a function as old as the history of inter-societal exchange relations of communities possessing or lacking typical resources. They are part and parcel of human ecosystem.The unmanageable and uncontrolled growth of any component of the ecosystem threatens its quality and endangers the balance among its components. It may then be said to be a source of pollution and may lead to de-generation of the natural and social fabric of a region. Then certain inherent attributes of market function may be taken as threat to environmental quality.

Locational and Functional Attributes

Hats and *bazaars* as key elements in environmental concerns may be examined from the standpoint of their locational and functional attributes. It may be seen that each market has a unique location with respect to natural and social environment it serves .The following locational examples may be generalized:

(i) Ox-bow lake and road/rail location
(ii) River channel and road/rail location
(iii) Tank-Temple road-junction location
(iv) Road/rail bridge over river location
(v) Transport node and forest side location
(vi) Forest side and road location
(vii) Power station and road-rail-river location
(viii) Road/rail and school, college/office location
(ix) Break-of-bulk point location, etc.

The environmental crisis stems from the normal functioning of *hats* and *bazaars* and may be multiplied with the locational attribute that has given rise to market functioning. For the present the pollution of land by *hats* and *bazaars* may be taken up first.

Locational Attributes

The locational attributes may be classified as:
(a) Water Bodies
(b) Forest
(c) Park/grove
(d) Infrastructure
(e) Social Facilities
(f) Human settlements

These may be given locational weightage like-

(a) Adjacent-3
(b) Near-2
(c) In vicinity-1

Functional Attributes

The functional attributes maybe classified according to the nature of goods involved in the sale of perishable goods and the respective residue left in the process of marketing at market places. For example the most common functions of routine use:

(a) Vegetable and fruits may leave a residue of 10gm/kg of their weight,
(b) Meat-20gm/kg,
(c) Fish-100gm/kg
(d) Chicken-200gm/kg

Similar to the weightage of locational attributes functional attributes for per kilogram residue may be worked out as under:

(a) Vegetable and fruit-0.05
(b) Meat and Fish-0.15
(c) Chicken-0.20
(d) Shop type-*gumti* –0.50 etc.

Composite Index

The scores of locational and functional attributes may be added to yield a composite index. The composite index may be reduced to a small figure by dividing the C.I. by 100.

Potential Land Pollution Index

In this way an index called Potential Land Pollution Index '(POLANPI INDEX)' (Shrivastava, V.K.1994) may be used to measure the potential land pollution due to *hats* and *bazaars* and serve as a measure of its de-generative impact on quality of environment. Retailing thus provides one of the means of observing and measuring the status of the health of the land. Land is a container of water so the quality of land has an impact on quality of water. Similarly air derives its components of dust, smoke, soot, humidity, and smell etc. from land. The status of lands is therefore, an indicator of the status of land, water and air—the three basic elements of environment.

It has been observed that the rank of POLANPI coincides with the hierarchical rank of *hats* and *bazaars*. It means that higher the order of market center higher the threat to environment in general. With the fast creeping consumerism due to globalization this threat must be accounted for, particularly in rural areas and remedial steps be undertaken.

REFERENCE

Shrivastava, V.K.(1994) Traditional Retailing and Environmental Pollution: A Case Study—India, in E. Terasaka and S. Takahashi (eds) *Comparative Study on Retail Trade Tradition and Innovation*, Ryutsu Keizai University, Japan.

3

Green Chemistry
A New Route to Protection of Environment

BINDU GANDHI, SADHNA SAXENA
and SEEMA TRIPATHI

Green chemistry refers to the programme of developing new chemical products and chemical processes for making improvements in the already existing compounds and processes so as to make them less harmful to human health and environment. Green chemistry is nothing to do with the chemistry of plants.

Green chemistry utilises the database information about the toxic and hazardous properties of certain chemicals in order to evaluate their positive and negative impact.

For attaining success in the objectives of green chemistry we have to keep in mind the following aspects—

1. Design chemical syntheses to prevent waste, leaving no waste to treat or cleanup.
2. Design safer and effective chemicals and products with no toxicity.
3. Design less hazardous syntheses to use and generate substances with little or no toxicity to humans and environment.
4. Use renewable feedstock (made from agricultural products' waste of other processes.).
5. Use catalysts not stoichiometric reagents. Catalysts are used in small amounts and carry out a single reaction

many times while reagents are used in excess and work only once.

6. Use catalysts not stoichiometric reagents. Catayst are used in small amounts and carry out a single reaction many times while reagents are used in excess and work only once.
7. Avoid chemical derivatives. Avoid using blocking or protecting groups or any temporary modification if possible. Derivatives use additional reagents and generate waste.
8. Maximize atom economy. Design syntheses so that the final product contains the maximum proportion of the staring material.
9. Use safer solvents and reaction conditions.
10. Increase energy efficiency. Run chemical reactions at ambient temperature and pressure whenever possible.
11. Design chemicals and products to degrade after use, so that they do not accumulate in the environment.
12. Analyse in real time to prevent pollution.
13. Design chemicals and their forms to minimise the potential for chemical accidents including explosions, fires and releases to the environment.

Chemists all over the world are using their skills to develop new processes, synthetic methods, analytical tools, reaction conditions, calalysts, etc.

Some achievements in this fields are:

1. Dense-phase carbon dioxide (Super Critical CO_2) has been recently developed chemical product. It is a wonderful material. It can be used as recyclable solvent and has number of applications in food industry.
2. Development of new method for synthesizing ibuprofen in 99 per cent yield. Avoiding use of large quantities of solvents and wastes associated with traditional methods.
3. In 1996 Dow Chemical used CO_2 as blowing agent for polystyrene foam production. Polystyrene foam is a

common material used in packing and food transportation. Seven hundred million pounds are produced each year in the United States alone.

Traditionally CFC and other ozone depleting chemicals were used in the production process of the foam sheets presenting a serious environmental problem. Dow chemical discovered that super critical CO_2 works equally well as blowing agent without the need for hazardous substances.

CO_2 used in the process is reused from other industries so the net carbon released from the process is zero.

4. Among many other green projects the development of oxidative cracking process is significant. It helps in production of ethylene, a major industrial raw material. This process saves about 13 trillion British thermal units of natural gas over conventional hydrocarbon cracking process. It also reduces carbon dioxide emissions by about four tonnes annually.

Thus green chemistry programmes accompolish pollution prevention in a cost effective manner.

4

Floriculture
An Initiative in Sustaining Ecology and Economy

KUMKUM RANI SHRIVASTAVA

The paper examines the role and potential of Self-Help Groups (SHG) in sustaining the economy and maintaining the ecology *pari passu*. Floriculture is one such activity in which rural women in particular may be involved in order to sustain the ecology and economy both. It is advocated that floriculture can be adopted as a means of empowering rural women, particularly housewives, who can utilize their off-the-work time in contributing towards family income and paying off the society in terms of sustaining the ecology.

The motivating force behind the idea depends on the hypotheses that:

(a) Rural housewives are in a position to spare at least a couple of hours from their routine work to undertake ventures like floriculture.
(b) The info-revolution has made them realize their work potential and their role in sustaining the ecology of the immediate environment.
(c) They possess the resources of time and energy that can be best utilized through floriculture activities accomplished on unutilized, vacant and barren patches of land adjacent to their dwellings.

(d) The dwelling environs are within their spatial reach and can be combined with the temporal freedom that they can avail and can productively utilize in between household obligations that they have to encounter.

The Indo-Nepal *tarai* region of Uttar Pradesh has great potential for floriculture due to its climatic character and availability of large *bhabhar* tracts which cannot be normally used for cultivation of crops. Maharaj Ganj District of Uttar Pradesh is one such example which lies in the *tarai* region and the northern part of the district comprises of *bhabhar* tracts. The climate of the region is of *monsoon* type. Due to relative proximity of the region to the Himalayan Mountain the moisture content of the air remains greater. The region is criss-crossed by river channels that carry water from the hills and at the break-of-slope point in *bhabhar* area they discharge much water, which spreads in the surrounding areas. Springs and swamps also characterize the area. A study of the agri-calendar of the area shows that from early May to mid September *kharif* crops couples with maize, *jowar* and *kodon-kutki* are cultivated. Further, from early October to early April the agri-scene is dominated by the cultivation of *rabi* crops like wheat, barley, pulses and mustard (Shrivastava, 2007). Floriculture flourishes in every season and in all kinds of enterprises be they professional cultivators or causal flower lovers. Similarly floriculture prospers on fertile and barren soils both.

Floral-calendar

Floral-calendar, unlike agri-calendar, is perpetual in nature. There is overlapping in floral-calendar. Even before the seasonal blossoming of a type of flower, the seeding of flowers of incoming season starts. This character makes perpetual availability of flowers possible. The continuous availability of flowers, on the other hand, generates stable flower markets. All flowers are beautiful and are able to prompt a sense of beauty. The sense of beauty comes from the heart and thus flowers may cultivate a feeling of love and compassion that excels material aspects of production, exchange and consumption. The domain of floriculture may become a medium to provide an access to human excellence. It is the human excellence, which can transform exploitative human actions to actions which may enhance, conserve and sustain the resource base of the earth and add to its longevity.

Floriculture Faith and Religion

Flowers are icons of faith and religion. Human adulation of the Supreme Being is offered through flowers. Flowers flow from gardens to markets and from markets to shrines and sanctuaries. The faith in the Supreme Being is expressed through the offerings of flowers. It is true for all kinds of religion found on the earth. This universal appeal of flowers attracts attention towards strengthening the culture of flowers.

Floriculture Beauty and Excellence

All flowers are beautiful. God creates all beautiful things. Flowers are, therefore, creation of the God through humans for their enrichment and sustained future. Floriculture is purposive. Its purpose is to cultivate a sense of fineness whereby a sense of geo-piety is created. This sagacity takes human beings beyond the goals of material achievements. It enlightens the human mind and drives it towards human excellence. Flowers and human excellence have a symbiotic relationship.

Self-Help Groups and Floriculture

Floriculture is not merely a type of agriculture or a type of informal economic activity. Floriculture is like the perennial income of a household, which knows no retirement. It is an uninterrupted human enterprise wherein the role of fair sex carries more weight. The examples have been met in the study region where about half a dozen women of different but almost adjacent houses have organized a system of flower cultivation without claiming any money from their families as input. Flowers grow naturally and on patches of land which are not specifically suitable to crops. This activity needs management of such patches of land and dedicates a couple of hours almost every day to take care of the blossoming buds. The collection of flowers and their offering to God is a prevalent practice in almost all households. Flowers have a tendency to blossom collectively and in large quantity if only a tender and caring hand is available. The growing number of flowers cannot be consumed in household offerings. Flowers are so beautiful and attractive that they cannot be disposed of as waste. They are voluntarily taken care of as they enrich the environment through their fragrance and enhance the beauty of those who are passionate to them. Women naturally fall ahead of man in this category.

Thus floriculture becomes adapted to women. Women are inborn managers. They manage the family of flowers and their kith and kin both. Thus floriculture becomes an enterprise run by women for men and God both. It has been noted that a couple of managers of the Self-Help Group belong to business family. They can help in locating to places from where flowers can be sent for forward trading. From village temple to community *puja* point and from there to town temple and onwards flower market has been identified and business may spread vertically. The members of the Self-Help Group have their own schedule to look after cultivation aspects of their enterprise. There are other members who look after processing, i.e. making garlands, bouquets, patchwork and so on. These activities are oriented to the nature and type of demand. With the growing sphere of information in rural areas the group members may be able to expand the activity.

Floriculture Model

The model envisaged to materialize a gender based enterprise almost wholly maintained and managed by rural women with nearly zero financial input together with the objective of clean environment and sustainable economy. It has been observed that a couple of rural household women have realized the merit of floriculture and they are practicing it remaining unknown from the fact that a widespread application of this concept can empower rural women and can enhance the quality of environment. This observation may be translated into a model that may be given effect in rural areas.

The model presumes that there are three Self-Help Groups involving around four to five female members of concerned households denoted by different symbols in Fig. 4.1. Each Self-Help Group members are engaged in managing flowers blooming naturally on the barren patches of vacant land around their hutments or houses. The consciousness about the beauty and utility of the flowers, which is inherent in entrepreneurial women, initiate flower cultivation in an organized manner. Flowers first of all find regular consumption in the rituals of village homes. Hence they do not go waste. Still all flowers blossoming so naturally may not be consumed. Secondly, the regular customer may be the village temple(s). With organized effort in order to best utilize their produce regular supply through combined collection of produce by the group members may be initiated. The task may be taken up by a couple of members of each Self-Help Group. Each of the members of the Self-Help Group may have either knowledge or expertise to collect and distribute their produce. The rest of the members of the Self-Help Group may manage production activity. The

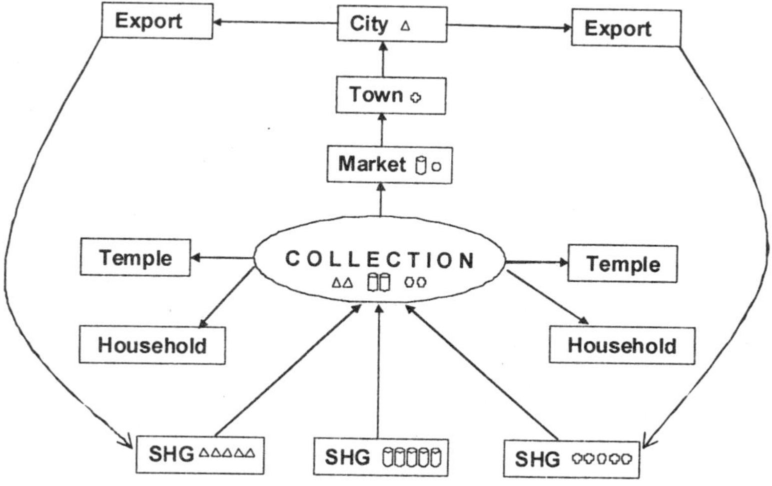

Fig. 4.1: Floriculture Model

natural outcome of combined production will be more quantity. Women possess an inbuilt mechanism for preservation, collection and sharing of utility produce. The self-help group members can plan a strategy of production, collection and utilization of flowers after fulfilling domestic needs and the needs of the local temple. They may interact with other self-help group members. Each self-help group may assign one or two of its skilled members to market the produce themselves. May be the self-help group members themselves join the sellers of other produce from their villages and start selling flowers without any intermediary. The feed back from self-help group member-sellers may help to explore better avenues of trade of flowers. Since, the members involved may be possessing different skills a couple of members of the self-help group may start exploring the avenues of consumption of the surplus flowers through village hats and bazaars up to town and city markets (Fig. 4.1). Since flowers are in large demand and are perishable links for their vertical transmission may be easily explored and executed. Flowers are in demand all over the world. It may not be surprising if scientific and demand oriented floriculture may open avenues of export of flowers to neighbouring countries. Export may generate feedback to promote empowerment of women.

By this time the self-help group have generated some money to cover the cost of transport, etc. The self-help group members may adapt to mobile conversation with traders at other *hats* and *bazaars* who may be in search of large quantity of flowers in towns and cities. The number of self-help group units may grow, get organized and reorient themselves to regular quality production of flowers and their trade after fulfilling domestic and local needs. The money so generated may be disbursed as income of the members who may, at this stage, be in a position to re-invest part of it in floriculture without creating any demand at any stage on their own family budget. Their earnings may be a bonus to the family.

REFERENCE

Shrivastava, V.K. (2007) *Periodic Markets and Agricultural Development*, Independent Publishers, New Delhi.

SECTION-B

DIMENSIONS OF ENVIRONMENTAL PROBLEMS

5

Perception of Environmental Problems
A Review

VANDANA MISHRA

This chapter reviews the nature of perception of environmental problems.

Looking at the world population, the number of people in various countries nursing the concern about environmental problems is very small. Included in them are some good-intentioned well-wishers of life, some yuppie environmentalists, some earth scientists and also some others searching simply for a new dish of academic problem. Why is the number so poor ?

Perhaps, the causes of environmental problems identified do not trigger the concern of larger mass of people. Of course, even of some of the so called educated people! Hence, a review of the causes is necessary.

The focus is on environmental problems. At the best, we expect that:

- Rainforests are not decimated;
- Water remains abundant and potable;
- Soils are not eroded and not poisoned chemically;
- The cover of ozone layer is not depleted;
- Inexorable melting of snowflakes is at least halted;
- Air pollution must be stopped or at last minimized.

But one needs to have a wider focus for the perception of environmental problems. Once this view is accepted, the scenario is bound to change. Therefore, the colour, the content and the context of the causes of environmental problems are bound to change, too.

Perceptive Base

The causes are results of the perceptive base of individuals or groups of them and they have their blind spots as well as tints.

Therefore, the causes of the environmental problems may be real and factual or socio-politically distorted or culturally tainted or existentially unaware. Therefore, a critical review is required.

The perceptive base of the causes (popularly talked of) lacks in the awareness of the existential considerations. It is limited to its appearance only. It is not wholistic. Therefore, the causes are superficial, though those are presented with good intentions. This is why people are doing things quite contrary to the cherished wishes for our ecosystem.

Modern Myths

The ongoing ouslaught of our earth's ingenious ecosystem is the result of the choices we have made or failed to make.

And the choices were made or could not be made because of the modern cultural values or myths. A few of them, as examples, may be considered to check the worth of the perceptive base and the related causes.

'Simplicity is barbarian or primitive while complexity is cultural or modern'. This concept has led to many of the ecological damages.

In distant past, there have been communities of highly evolved human beings. They lived the culture of simplicity. They were never tempted by complexities. Hence, there were no damages to the ecosystem.

Have our "causes" taken this fact into consideration?

Our modern culture puts total emphasis on *"doingness"*. It neglects *"beingness"*. The unavoidable result is "the monkey became man but man has remained monkey" (OSHO).

And this man is being trained to achieve, to accomplish, to get ahead, to rise to the top, to be successful, to do things that bring "fame and fortune" whether it is of value or not. People as well as nations are being told to do these things even at the cost of throat-cut competition, drudgery, overtime, pressure, tension, nervous breakdown, heart-attack and wars between nations behind this or that guise.

And this man is expected to do things that will save and improve the ecosystem.

So, unless people are helped to rise to higher consciousness, we cannot stop the killing of our ecosystem.

At least one more aspect of our modern culture is worth considering. It is directly related to the problems of our environment. Some of our ideas of culture have promoted the state that society is becoming the product of technology. Hence, technology is outwitting human intelligence to use its products for good. If technology is shaped to be the product of society, the story would be different. It would be more humane and in communion with cosmology. Is not cosmology the greatest technology ? Then, why not go with it.

6

Air Pollution

SAVITA KANWAR

The chapter deals with the contamination of air by the discharge of harmful substances, identifies the causes and suggests remedies for clean air and green environs.

One of the formal definitions of air pollution is as follows—"The presence in the atmosphere of one or more contaminants in such quality and for such duration as is injurious, or tends to be injurious, to human health or welfare, animal or plant life." It is well known that air pollution can cause health problems and it can also damage the environment and property. It has also lead to thinning of the protective ozone layer of the atmosphere which may result in human health hazards. Air pollution has increased over the years due to modernization and progress. Some of the major factors of air pollution are industries, vehicles, increase in population and urbanization etc. Air pollution can be due to many reasons, some of which are not within human control.

Pollutants and Their Causes

Carbon monoxide (CO_2) is a colourless, odourless gas that is produced by the incomplete burning of carbon-based fuels including petrol, diesel, and wood. It is also produced from the combustion of natural and synthetic products such as cigarettes. It lowers the amount of oxygen that enters our blood. It can slow our reflexes and make us confused and sleepy.

Carbon dioxide(CO_2) is the principle greenhouse gas emitted as a result of human activities such as the burning of coal, oil, and natural gases.

Chlorofluorocarbons (CFC) are gases that are released mainly from air-conditioning systems and refrigeration. When released into the air, CFCs rise to the stratosphere, where they come in contact with few other gases, which lead to reduction of the ozone layer that protects the earth from the harmful ultraviolet rays of the sun.

Lead is present in petrol, diesel, lead batteries, paints, hair dye products, etc. Lead affects children in particular. It can cause nervous system damage and digestive problems and, in some cases, cause cancer.

Ozone gas occurs naturally in the upper layers of the atmosphere. This important gas shields the earth from the harmful ultraviolet rays of the Sun. However, at the ground level, it is a pollutant with highly toxic effects. Vehicles and industries are the major source of ground-level ozone emissions. Ozone makes our eyes itch, burn and water. It also lowers our resistance to colds and pneumonia.

Nitrogen oxide causes smog and acid rain. It is produced from burning fuels including petrol, diesel, and coal. Nitrogen oxides can make children susceptible to respiratory diseases in winters.

Suspended Particulate Matter (SPM) consists of solids in the air in the form of smoke, dust and vapor that can remain suspended for extended periods and is also the main source of haze that reduces visibility. The finer of these particles, when breathed in can lodge in our lungs and cause lung damage and respiratory problems.

Sulphur dioxide (SO_2) is a gas produced from burning coal, mainly in thermal power plants. Some industrial processes, such as production of paper and smelting of metals, produce sulphur dioxide. It is a major contributor to smog and acid rain. Sulfur dioxide can lead to lung diseases.

Acid rain is due to air pollution. The phenomenon occurs when sulphur dioxide and nitrogen oxides from the burning of fossil fuels such as, petrol, diesel and coal combine with water vapor in the atmosphere and fall as rain, snow and fog. These gases can also be emitted from natural sources like volcanoes. Acid rain causes extensive damage to water, forest, soil resources and even human health.

Smog is a combination of various gases with vapor and dust. Smog can affect urban fringe and rural areas as well as big cities. Its occurrences are often linked with heavy traffic, high temperatures and calm winds. During the winter, wind speeds are low and cause the smoke and fog to stagnate, hence pollution levels can increase near ground level. This keeps the pollution close to the ground, right where people are breathing. It hampers visibility and harms the environment. *Heavy smog greatly decreases ultraviolet radiation.*

Fly ash consists of silica, alumina, oxides of iron, calcium and magnesium and toxic heavy metals like lead, arsenic, cobalt and copper. Fly ash lowers soil fertility and contaminates surface and ground water as it can leach into the subsoil. When siltation fly ash gets into the natural draining system, it results in and clogs the system. It also reduces the pH balance and portability of water. Fly ash interferes with the process of photosynthesis of aquatic plants and thus disturbs the food chain. Besides, fly ash corrodes exposed metallic structures in its vicinity.

Indoor air pollution refers to the physical, chemical and biological characteristics of air in the indoor environment within a home, building, or an institution or commercial facility.

Volatile organic compounds originate mainly from solvents and chemicals. The main indoor sources are perfumes, hair sprays, furniture polish, glues, air fresheners, moth repellents, wood preservatives and many other products used in the house. The main health effect is the irritation of the eye, nose and throat. In more severe cases there may be headaches, nausea and loss of coordination. In the long term, some of the pollutants are suspected to bring damage to the liver and other parts of the body.

Tobacco smoke generates a wide range of harmful chemicals and is known to cause cancer and it is well known that passive smoking causes a wide range of problems to the passive smoker (the person who is in the same room with a smoker and is not himself/herself a smoker) ranging from burning eyes, nose and throat irritation to cancer, bronchitis, severe asthma and a decrease in lung function.

Pesticides, if used carefully and the manufacturer's, instructions followed carefully do not cause too much harm to the indoor air.

Biological pollutants include pollen from plants, mite, hair from pets, fungi, parasites and some bacteria. Most of them are allergens and can cause asthma, hay fever and other allergic diseases.

Formaldehyde is a gas that comes mainly from carpets, particle boards and insulation foam. It causes irritation to the eyes and nose and may cause allergies in some people.

Asbestos is mainly a concern in air pollution because it is suspected to cause cancer.

Radon is a gas that is emitted naturally by the soil. Due to modern houses having poor ventilation, it is confined inside the house causing harm to the dwellers.

Impact of Air Pollution

Air pollutants have serious impact on human health affecting the lungs and the respiratory system, they are also taken up by the blood and pumped all round the body. These pollutants are also deposited on soil, plants and in the water, further contributing to human exposure.

Moderating the Impact of Air Pollution

Some steps that can help reduce air pollution are:

- Morning walk and jogging
- Ride more bicycle.
- Public transports should be used as much as possible.
- Plant more trees and look after them.

- Share air conditioners and coolers and fans.
- Aerosols should not be used in household.
- Leaves should be used to make manure.
- Use only unleaded petrol.
- One should regularly check the pollution level of our cars and they should be fitted with catalytic converters.

7

Air Pollution by Carbonmonoxide and Its Consequences

SANJAY PRABHUNE, RAJSHRI SOMANI and V. NILOSEY

Introduction

Air pollutants are present in the atmosphere in concentrations that disturb the dynamic equilibrium in the atmosphere and thereby affect man and his environment. Therefore air is never found clean in nature. Gases such as CO, SO_2 and H_2S are continually released into the atmosphere through natural activities, e.g. volcanic activity, vegetation decay and forest fires. Besides, tiny particles of solids or liquids are distributed throughout the air by winds, volcanic explosions and other similar natural disturbances. In addition to these 'natural pollutants', there are man-made pollutants-gases, mist, fog, and particulates, aerosols—resulting from the chemical and biological process used by man. The latter are present in relatively high concentrations compared to the background values in air. These pollutants hardly exist beyond 600 m. above ground level.

Primary Pollutants

There are five primary pollutants which together contribute more than 90 per cent of global air pollution. These are:

(A) Carbon Monoxide, CO
(B) Nitrogen oxides, NO_x

(C) Hydrocarbons, HC
(D) Sulphur oxides, SO_x
(E) Particulates, part

Transportation activity accounts for more than 46 per cent of the total pollutants produced per year and hence remains the principal source of air pollution. Carbon monoxide is the major individual pollutant with a tonnage matching that of all other pollutants together. It may be noted, however, that evaluation of pollutants and sources in terms of tonnage does not give the correct picture since a minor pollutant can be much more dangerous than a major pollutant. Thus, particulate pollutants are the most dangerous among the primary pollutants listed in Table 7.1 (relative toxicity—particulate = 107 compared to CO = 1).

Carbon Monoxide Pollution Sources

It is a colourless, odourless and tasteless gas above –192°C (–314°F). It is 96.5 per cent as heavy as air and is not soluble in water. The basic chemical reactions yielding CO are :

1. Incomplete combusition of fuel or carbon-containing compounds :
   $2C + O_2 \rightarrow 2CO$
   $CO_2 + C \rightarrow 2CO$
2. Dissociation of CO_2 at high temperatures:
   $CO_2 \rightarrow CO + O$

Sources and Sinks of CO Pollution

Natural processes, e.g. volcanic action, natural gas emission, electrical discharge during storms, seed germination, marsh-gas production, etc. contributed in a small measure to CO in the atmosphere. The significant contribution is from human activities. The annual emission on a global scale is 350 million tonnes (human source 275 and natural 75 million tonnes). (A) Transportation contributes about 64 per cent of CO-motor vehicles, 59.2 per cent; aircrafts 2.4 per cent; and railoads

Table 7.1: Primary Pollutant Sources and Amounts (million tonnes/year-1)

Pollutant	*Weight of Pollutant produced*						*Total weight of pollutant produced by each source*
	CO	*NOx*	*HC*	*SOx*	*Part <20*	*>3*	
Transportation	69.7	10.1	10.8	0.8	1.2	1.0	93.6
Fuel combustion (Stationery Sources)	1.2	11.8	1.4	21.9	4.6	1.3	42.2
Industrial Processes	7.8	0.7	9.4	4.1	6.3	2.7	31.0
Solid-waste disposal	7.8	0.6	1.6	0.1	1.1	—	11.2
Miscellaneous	8.5	0.4	6.3	0.1	1.3	—	16.6
Total weight of each pollutant produced	95.0	23.6	29.5	27.0		19.5	194.6

Note : National Air Quantity and Emissions trends Report, Research Triangle Park.

0.1 per cent. (B) Next in magnitude is miscellaneous sources, 16.9 per cent—the main components are forest fires, 7.2 per cent and agricultural burning, 8.3 per cent. Agricultural burning implies controlled burning of forest debris, crop residues, brush, weeds and other vegetation. (C) Industrial processes, mainly iron, steel industries, petroleum and paper industries, constitute the third largest contributor of CO (9.6%) to the air. The atmospheric background of CO is 0.1 ppm.

Sinks

The annual input of CO into the atmosphere by human activities is expected to double its concentration in the ambient (surrounding) atmosphere every five years. But the actual increase in ambient global CO concentration is much less. The major CO sink is some soil microorganisms. A potting soil sample weighing 2.8 kg completely removed, in three hours, 120 ppm CO from ambient air.

The same soil sample, when sterilized, failed to remove CO from air. 200 microorganisms isolated from the soil and cultured, 16 fungi were found to be active in the removal of CO.

Concentration Profile

The soil sinks can take care of atmospheric CO, but it still exists in significant concentrations in the atmosphere. This is because neither CO nor the soil sink is distributed uniformly. As a matter of fact, the largest CO producing areas often have the least amount of soil sink available.

Since the automobile remains the largest single source of CO pollutant (59.2%), highly populated urban areas have the highest ambient CO concentrations.

Effects of Carbon Monoxide Pollution

Carbon monoxide gas comes in the atmosphere by various method. Some of them are natural processes and some by human activity.

But these causes very harmful effect to the living bodies.

Effect of Carbon Monoxide on Living Beings

Human body consists a liquid called blood. This is red in colour. the red colour of blood is due to the presence of a pigment called hemoglobin. This hemoglobin pigment contains iron (Fe). Due to the iron it is red in colour.

But the main function of this hemoglobin is to supply the oxygen to the all parts of the body. For this, blood continually goes to the lungs and takes fresh oxygen. As a result of this it forms a temporary compound called Ox hemoglobin. So this Ox hemoglobin reaches the body parts and gives oxygen. When this oxygen given to the body part as a result of this oxygen and hemoglobin break.

This is more clear by the help of reactions:

(i) Hemoglobin → Lungs → Ox hemoglobin.

(in the blood) (Oxygen) (temporary compound)

$He + O_2 \rightarrow HeO_2$

(ii) Ox hemoglobin → Oxygen → Hemoglobin→
He O_2——————> He + O_2
(In body part)
Here : He = Hemoglobin

At the same time when Ox hemoglobin breaks into the oxygen and hemoglobin that hemoglobin attaches to the carbon dioxide present in the body part (produced due to the metabolisim) and this new compound again goes to the lungs. At the lungs this carbon dioxide break from hemoglobin and this carbon dioxide goes out of body by the process of respiration.

But the most important thing is that the attachment of the oxygen and carbon dioxide to the hemoglobin is a temporary process. When the concentration of the carbon monoxide is high in the air at that time intake air taken for respiration contains much more carbon monoxide. When this carbon monoxide comes in contact of hemoglobin it forms a compound called carbaminohemoglobin. But the most harmful thing is that the attachment of carbon monoxide to the hemoglobin is not temporary.

Consequently, the use of that hemoglobin molecule is stopped and that hemoglobin molecule is not further used. If the amount of the carbon monoxide in air is very high and that air is inhered for respiration at that time it causes fits and other serious problems.

Reaction

Hemoglobin + Carbon monoxide → Carbaminohemoglobin (Permanent Compound)

The carbon of carbon monoxide acts as soft base. It forms much stronger bond with border line acid Fe^{2+} in comparison to hard base O^{2-}. Thus CO is a very toxic substance.

Effect of Carbon Monoxide on Plants

Plants perform a process of production of oxygen called photosynthesis. In the presence of sunlight, chlorophyll, water, and carbondioxide plant body produces fresh oxygen. For this process plant leaves have small holes in them called stomata. From these stomata carbon dioxide goes inside the plant as a raw material for photosynthesis.

But when the concentration of carbon monoxide high in the air at that time it goes into the stomata and the process of production of fresh oxygen fails. As a result of this production of oxygen suffers.

Effect of Carbon Monoxide on Soils

Carbon monoxide comes from vehicles. When comes in contact with soil it forms a thin layer of carbon particles on it. As a result of this fertility of soils is lost.

REFERENCES

1. Anil Kumar De, *Environmental Chemistry*, Third Edition, May, 1994, Wiley Eastern Ltd. New Age International Limited, pp. 102, 104, 105, 299, 300, 301, 154, 110, 109, 108, 107, 106.
2. J.O'M. Bockris, *Environmental Chemistry*, Plenum Press, New York and London 1977, pp. 218, 219, 220.
3. S.M. Khopkar, *Environmental Pollution Analysis*, pp. 61, 62, 76, 77.
4. *Encyclopedia of Environmental Pollution*.

8

Thermal Pollution

ALKA NEEMA

Introduction

Thermal pollution is a by-product of rapid and unplanned industrial progress and over population. It indicates the detrimental effect of heated effluents discharged by various power plants. It impairs the quality and deteriorates the aquatic and terrestrial environments.

Sources of Thermal Pollution

Human activities are constantly adding pollutants to air and water at an alarming rate. Following sources contribute to thermal pollution:

1. **Nuclear power plants:** Nuclear power plants, research institutes, nuclear experiments and explosions, discharge of a lot of unutilized heat and toxic radio nuclides into nearby water streams. The power reactor and the nuclear fuel processing units are the major contributor of heat in the aquatic environment. The liquid radioactive water consists of H-3, C-14, Fe-59 and Co-60 along with corrosive products. In addition, accidental leakages of radiation from nuclear reactors in water raise the temperature of surrounding aquatic system and severely affect the aquatic flora and fauna.
2. **Coal-fired power plants:** These constitute the major source of thermal pollutants. Their condenser coils are

cooled with water from nearby lake or river and discharge the hot water back into the water, killing fish and other marine organisms. (15°C higher) back to the stream. This decreases the dissolved Oxygen (D 0) content of water, killing fish and other marine organisms.

3. **Industrial effluents:** Industries like electricity-generating, textile, pulp paper, sugar, etc. require huge amount of cooling water for heat removal. To cope with the tremendous demands of electricity, the efficiency of the turbine is increased by creating a partial vacuum at its exhaust by cooling and condensing the turbine steam. In modern station a producing 100 M.W. nearly one million gallons are discharged in an hour which increases the temperature of cooling water by 8 to 10°C.
4. **Domestic sewage:** Municipal sewage commonly discharged into rivers normally has a higher temperature than the receiving water. Besides increasing the temperature, the organic matter present in the sewage utilizes the dissolved oxygen present in the surface water for oxidation. Demand of oxygen increases. Hence, the anaerobic condition is set up resulting in the release of foul and offensive gases in water. The marine organisms depending on dissolved oxygen of the surface water die out.
5. **Hydro-electric power:** Generation of hydro-electric power sometimes results in negative thermal loading in water system. It has been reported that about 18 per cent more heat is given to cooling water in nuclear power plants than any other plant of equivalent size.

Thermal Power Plant Pollution

India depends mostly on coal to generate electricity. An enormous environmental damage is caused by the combustion of coal. High ash content of Indian coal means more wear and tear of the plant and machinery, low thermal efficiency of the boiler, slogging, choking and sealing of furnaces and tubing and most serious of all generation of large amount of slag and fly ash. The solid wastes run into the nearby stream choke the natural drainage system and despoil the land down stream. Hence, fly ash finds its way onto coastal plains, producing siltation and increasing flood hazards. The fallout fly ash increases the suspended particle matter in the air and adversely affects the agricultural lands, flora and vegetation in the surrounding areas. The gases SO_2 and Nitrogen oxide pollutes the atmosphere. They cause acid rain, which is responsible for the damage of soil, vegetation and aquatic of life of region.

Fly ash has a hazardous effect. An important feature of it is that as the concentration of metals increases the size of the particle decreases. When inhaled 10 to 1 micron size particle it causes the disease known as silicosis. Considering huge consumption of coal in thermal plants, even a small fraction of the halogens present enters into such reaction; the generation of CFCs (chlorofluoro carbons) will be so large that the present world consumption of industrial CFCs would be very small.

A holistic analysis of the long-term global impact of hydrocarbon burning is the combustion of atmospheric oxygen and production of CO_2 in the process. Thus in the burning process of the fossil fuel burning 3 tonnes of carbon will consume 8 tonnes of oxygen and hence we are borrowing from the present oxygen reserve of the atmosphere. Exposure to fly ash affects the bones and lungs. Therefore, the next time when we switch on any electrical appliance, we should also remember its environmental impacts.

Harmful Effects of Thermal Pollutants

1. **Reduction of Dissolved Oxygen:** D O concentration in water—is 14.6ppm in water at 31°F and 6.6ppm at 64°F. So, aquatic animals cannot survive.
2. **Change in Water Properties:** Decrease in density, viscosity and solubility of gases and increase in settling speed of suspended particles, seriously affect the food supplies of aquatic organisms.
3. **Increase in Toxicity:** Increase of the toxic effect of KCN and Oxylene causes massive mortality of fish.
4. **Interference with Biological Activities:** Life process of aquatic animals involves several chemical reactions

and rate of these reactions vary according to the change in temperature.

5. **Interference with Reproduction:** The maximum temperature of spawning successfully is 8.9°C. The warm water destroys the laid eggs. There is variation in reproduction rate, change in metabolic rate, increased vulnerability to disease, invasion of destructive organism, etc. is caused by hot water.
6. **Undesired Changes in Algae Population:** High water temperatures promote blue green algal blooms, which disrupt the aquatic food chains.
7. **Increasing Biochemical Oxygen Demand and Affecting Distribution of Organisms:** Aquatic organisms move towards suitable temperature and their activities are influenced by the change in density, surface tension, viscosity of water, etc. For example, planktonic organisms cannot compensate for pull of gravity in less dense water and ultimately sink.

Thermal Effects on Man and His Environment

Human body temperature (35 to 40°C) is close to optimum temperature (37 to 40°C) of pathogens. Heated effluents from various sources enhance the reproduction or harmful microorganisms like thermophiles and mesophiles. Condenser effluents raise the temperature of water and catalyze chemical degradation, the contaminated flow is saturated with toxic pollutants containing less oxygen making the water unfit for any purpose. Replicated human pathogens spread infectious diseases in man. Blue green algae also grow rapidly, deteriorating the quality of water rendering it unsuitable for human consumption.

1. Selecting the suitable site for setting up the thermal power stations coupled with effective use of regulated river system.
2. Channeling the thermal effluents.
3. Using adequate cooling towers or ponds or artificial lakes.

4. Efficient designing or outfalls to prevent thermal blocking.
5. Avoiding interferences of hot water mass with fish migration.
6. Heat transport mechanisms, like advection and dispersion or turbulent mixing should be considered to prevent pollution.
7. Temperature prediction models can be used to the safe engineered designs.
8. By improving the efficiencies of electric power generating plants.

Measurement of Thermal Pollution

The parameters and instruments used for measuring thermal pollutants include:

1. *Determination of physical parameters* such as temperature distribution, DO concentration and Lux readings.
2. *Electronic temperature meter.* In this, reversing thermometers, resisting thermometers, thermocouples and thermistors are employed to measure temperature at different depths.
3. *Dissolved oxygen meters*: DO determination can be done by direct reading portable equipment.
4. *Lux meter*: It consists of a photosensitive detector which measures to photo current and the extent of thermal effluents discharged in the water. It shows the depth up to which sun light penetration is decreased due to impurities, turbidity and pollutants in water. The instrument is provided with 0-50, 0-500 and 0-5000 Lux.

Conclusion

The earth, our future—just save it. Let us take a pledge to safe guard Mother Earth.

9

Air Pollution Sources, Causes and Prevention

Jyoti Doodhiya, Anamika Jain

The presence of one or more contaminates in the atmosphere in such quantities and for such time as injurious or tends to be injurious to human health or to the welfare of animal or plant life is known as air pollution.

It is known that air pollution results from a variety of causes, not all of which are within human control (Table 9.1). Dust storms in desert areas and smoke from forest and grass fires contribute to chemical and particulate pollution of the air. The substances that pollute the atmosphere are gases, finely divided solid or finely dispersed liquid aerosols.

Some of the air pollutants, which are discharged into the air are carbon compounds like carbon monoxide, etc., the largest source of air pollution in automotive exhaust fumes. Burning of fossil fuel results in the emission of carbon dioxide, carbon dioxide is the main greenhouse gas. Due to the greenhouse effect the temperature of the earth is rising day by day.

Nitrogen oxides that are emitted from burning fuels, sulphur oxides are formed during burning coal in thermal power plants. Some industrial processes such as production of paper and smelting of metals also produce sulphur oxide.

The combustion of gasoline for engines or for heating releases hydrocarbons.

Lead is a very potent air pollutant, it is present in petrol, diesel, paints etc. It can cause damage to our nervous system. Thermal power generation through the combination of coal produces minute particles of ash that causes serious environmental problems. These particles consist of silica, alumina, oxides of iron, calcium and magnesium.

Chlorofluorocarbons (CFCs) are used for air conditioning and refrigeration systems. The presence of CFCs in the atmosphere is responsible for the depletion of ozone layer, producing a 'hole' in it.

The most important natural source of air pollution is volcanic activity, which at times releases large amounts of ash and toxic fumes into the atmosphere. Petroleum refinery of Mathura is an example of air pollution, which is responsible for the corrosion of the historical monuments like Taj Mahal and Fatehpur Sikri.

Control and Prevention of Air Pollution

The best way to protect air quality is to reduce pollutant emission by changing to fuels and processes that are less polluting.

Air pollution due to vehicles can be controlled by reducing the emissions from the vehicles. For this one must use unleaded petrol, and even the engines are designed in a manner that leads to complete elimination of the most harmful gases, carbon monoxide. Removing particulate matter and gaseous polluants can reduce air pollution due to industries, power plants, mills and plants. Use the less polluting forms of power generation, such as solar energy or wind energy. Use of other forms of renewable energy may also be explored. Lead free fuel such as Compressed Natural Gas (CNG) should be used for running cars, buses, etc. Grow more trees.

Thus all of us must take appropriate steps and observe restraints to contribute in keeping the air around us clean and healthy.

Table 9.1: Artificial Pollutants and Their Sources

S. No.	*Source*	*Main Pollutants*
1	Domestic combustion of fuels like coal, wood and oil, Cigarettes.	Smoke, CO, CO_2, SO_2, metallic oxides, oxides, 4% Co, 0.5 µg of lead per cigarette, NO_x
2	Power Generation —Thermal power plants —Nuclear power plants —Hydro power plants —Diesel generators	Smoke, CO, CO_2, SO_2, dusts, radio-active compound like I-131, Argon-41, Sr-90, Cs-137, C-14 etc. Methane as marshy gas from water-logged areas.HC, CO, NO_x, Noise
3	Incinerators —Open burning —Commercial, municipal and industrial incinerators.	Smoke, CO, NO_x and flyash
4	Petroleum refineries —Boilers, process heaters and regenerators. —Reactors, storage tanks, compressor, generators.	Noise, SO_x, HC
5	Inorganic chemical and fertilizer manufacturing	SPM, noise, odour, HF, NH_3, H_3PO_4 and acid mists
6	Organic chemical manufacturing: plastics, paints, varnishes, rubber, pesticides, insecticides, soaps and detergents, phenols, methanol, alcohol etc.	SPM, noise, odour, SO_x, CO, gases and vapours
7	Pulp and paper manufacturing: Blowers washer, furnaces, evaporators oxidation towers.	Mercaptans, SO_2, SPM, noise, odour, H_2S.
8	Agriculture —Ploughing —Crop sprayig and dusting —Field burning	Dusts and odours insecticides, pesticides,chlorinated hydrocarbons, lead, arsenic, phosphates Smoke, flyash, soot
9	Food processing: Drying, preserving and packaging	Dusts, vapours, odours
10	Transportation: Bullock carts, motor vehicles, cars, trucks, aircrafts, trains	HCs and CO (95% of total Co and HCs are from transportation only) lead, dusts, noise, NO_x, and rubber and evaporative emissions like olefins, paraffins, aroma tics, benzene etc.

S. No.	Source	Main Pollutants
11	Roasting and heating processes of non metallic minerals: Crushed stone, gravel sand processing, cement, glass, refectories, ceramics, manufacturing, coal clearing.	Minerals and organics SPM, SO_x, NO_x, dusts.
12	Ferrous metallurgical material handling, ore sintering and pelletising, coke ovens, blast furnaces, steel furnaces.	Smoke fumes, Co, odours, H_2S, vapours, florides.
13	Non-ferrous metallurgical processes	Dusts fumes of Cu, Zn etc.
14	Roasting, smelting and refining	SO_x

10

Environmental Pollution with Special Reference to Toxic Effects of Various Chemicals

DIPANITA GARGAVA

Environment can be defined as the sum-total of all biotic and biotic components that are present on the earth including man. Environmental pollution and the problems related to it are the burning issues that the world is facing today. Man-made activities are resulting in the deterioration of the environment and its resources. This is a matter of great global concern, which needs quick remedy otherwise the consequences, will be disastrous.

A wave of concern for the environment swept across the developed countries in the sixties and reached the climax in 1970 with the celebration of "Earth Day" under the auspices of the United Nations. Then from 1972 onwards with the conclusion of the United Nations Conference on Human Environment at Stockholm. This wave started sweeping across India and other developing countries. The need for environmental education, both formal and informal, was keenly felt at the national level. The objective of environmental education was to enlighten the public about the protection and conservation of our environment and the need to restrain human activities which lead to indiscriminate release of pollutants into the environment.

The chapter explains natural and man induced causes of environmental pollution and elaborates upon the toxic effects of various chemicals.

Causes of Environmental Pollution

Population growth, air and water pollution from industrial activities, conversion of forest land for agriculture, settlements and industry and undesirable development are some of the major causes of the environmental pollution that the world is facing today. It is for these reasons that the quality of environment has deteriorated and has become unfavourable to human health and other forms of biotic life. The main causes of environmental pollution can be grouped under two heads, i.e. natural disasters and man induced disasters.

Natural Disasters

Floods: Floods bring great disaster to the environment. They cause uprooting of trees thereby causing soil erosion, destruction of flora and fauna, epidemics, loss of life and property, etc.

Earthquakes: Cause destruction of land, dismantling of buildings and roads, loss of lives, property, etc.

Storms and Cyclones: High speed winds uproot trees, destroy crops, results in loss of top soil thereby decreasing the fertility of agricultural land and also causing various types of environmental pollutions.

Landslides: Landslides occurring in the mountainous regions remove the top soil as well as the vegetation in that particular area there-by causing soil erosion and loss of humus.

Man Induced Disasters

Deforestation: Regular cutting of trees especially in the forest areas not only causes damage to the soil but also decreases its fertility. Rainfall is affected and the biodiversity suffers great loss due to destruction of habitat.

Uneconomical Use of Resources: The pressure of population on both renewable and non-renewable resources has brought irreversible damage to the environment. With population growth the demand for more land, water and more consumption has increased so much that there are not enough resources to go around.

Fishing Activity: Fishing is one of the oldest industries that man has known and various fishing practices are followed in different parts of the world. The global fishing fleet is estimated to be 250 per cent larger than needed to catch what the ocean can produce. It is only now that people are waking up to the environmental impact of fishing and how it affects the ecosystem of the oceans.

Tourism: Tourism is one activity which is contributing to environmental pollution on a large scale. It causes air emissions, solid waste, litter, noise, oil and chemical, and the release of sewage.

Coal Mining: Coal is still one of the major sources of energy in the developing and developed world. The coal mines not only cause environmental damage but also have an adverse effect on the health of the workers and of the surrounding population. Burning coal also releases tons of pollutants like carbon dioxide (a major cause of global warming) and sulphur dioxide (a cause of acid rain) into the atmosphere.

Rapid Urbanization: Rapid urbanization burdens the land with a lot of problems. There is excessive consumption of resources, encroachment of land for secondary and tertiary activities, loss of vegetation, water scarcity, energy demand, pollution etc.

Hunting and Poaching: This activity leads to the loss of animal life and ultimately disturbs the ecological balance.

Excessive use of Insecticides, Pesticides and Herbicides: The use of chemicals for enhancing yield of crops indirectly toxicities the soil. Harmful chemicals enter into the soils and from there into the food chain.

Extensive Grazing: Excessive grazing causes reduction in the nutrients present in the soil leading to low productivity as well as soil erosion.

Increase of Toxic Chemicals and Gases in the Environment: Excessive burning of fuel, waste from industries, smoke emitted from vehicles, excessive use of chemicals in fertilizers and manures increases the toxic chemicals in the atmosphere.

Effects of Environmental Pollution

Attention may now be paid to the effects of environmental pollution.

Consumption of Chemicals: The production, trade, use, and release of synthetic chemicals are now widely recognized as a global threat to human health and environmental pollution. Yet, the world's chemical industries continue to produce and release thousands of chemical compounds every year, in most cases with none or very little testing and understanding of their impact on people and the environment.

Scientists estimate that due to the presence of effluents in rivers, toxic waste dumps in fields, poisons in groundwater, in the air , in food, all living species today carry at least 700 man-made chemical contaminants in their bodies. These chemicals are implicated in effects in living beings ranging from the gory to the subtle-from gross effects like cancers, deformed sex organs and hermaphroditic to hidden consequences such as falling sperm counts, aggressive behaviour and diminished intelligence.Toxic and nontoxic chemicals are present in the environment. The toxic chemicals are discharged by industries into air, water and soil. They get into the human food chain and disturb the biochemical process. No one knows how many chemicals contaminate our bodies but more that 100 is a conservative estimate. Their combined effect on health and the environment is largely unknown.

For years the chemical industry has persuaded governments that the risks posed by chemicals are too small to worry about and governments have assured that existing legislation provides adequate protection. But growing evidence suggests otherwise. So great is the number of chemicals all around us that we're constantly exposed to multiple doses— the combined effect of which could be affecting our health. There is particular concern about the risks to children and babies since they are the most vulnerable. Some of these hazardous chemicals are known to affect the development of babies—even inside the womb. Chemicals released into our environment now will go on having an effect.

***Nuclear Tests*:** Nuclear tests in populated areas cause heavy destruction claiming thousands of lives and also cause harm to the resources.

***E-Waste*:** India along with other Asian countries like Pakistan and China are increasingly becoming a dumping ground for hazardous wastes from old computers and electronic items, The electronic waste contains several hazardous and toxic materials like lead, mercury, cadmium, PVC, plastics and ruminated flame retardants, which are known to cause severe defects in human bodies. The electronics industry is often considered a 'clean' industry. But sleek shiny gadgets hide a darker side of the industry. Some of the electronics industries biggest brands, and their suppliers, are contaminating rivers and underground wells with a wide range of hazardous chemicals during production.

***Toxic Chemicals*:** Toxic chemicals may be classified according to their functions. There are four million known chemicals in the world and another 30,000 new compounds are added to the list every year. Chemicals like Be, Cd, benzene, asbestos, arsenic, zinc, copper, boron etc are present in air and water. Water bodies contain a large amount of pesticides from the drainage of agricultural land.

***Impact of Toxic Chemicals on Enzymes*:** Toxic chemicals attack active sites of enzymes inhibiting essential enzyme function. Hg^{2+}, Pb^{2+} and Cd^{2+} act as effective enzyme inhibitors.

***Biochemical Effect of Arsenic*:** Arsenic occurring in fungicides, herbicides and insecticides attack the Self-Help Group of enzymes thereby inhibiting enzyme action.

***Biochemical Effect of Cadmium*:** Cadmium occurs with zinc minerals. Growing plants acquire cadmium along with zinc. Cadmium poisoning leads to ouch disease in which bones become fragile. Kidney problems, anemia and bone marrow disease result due to high-level cadmium in the body.

***Biochemical Effect of Lead*:** Street dusts and roadside soil are enriched with Pb which moves into our body along with our diet. It leads to hematological damage and hinders harem synthesis.

Biochemical Effect of Mercury: Effects of mercury a well known toxic metal came into limelight only after Minima incident in 1953 in Japan. Many lost their lives or were paralyzed after consuming mercury-contaminated fish. Genetic disorders were also found.

Hg or its salts can be converted to methyl mercury by anaerobic methane synthesizing bacteria in water. This is consumed by photo planktons and enters into the food chain.

Biochemical Effects of Carbon Monoxide: Approximately 530 tonnes of CO is present in the atmosphere. Carbon monoxide attacks hemoglobin and displaces oxygen to form carboxyl hemoglobin. This reduces the blood's capacity for carrying oxygen thereby causing metabolic disorders and ending in death.

Biochemical Effects of Nitrogen Oxides: Nitric oxide like CO forms a bond with hemoglobin and reduces oxygen transport efficiency posing health hazards.

Biochemical Effects of Sulphur Dioxide: Sulphur dioxide responsible for air pollution has an effect on respiratory tract, causing irritation and increasing air resistance. Sulphur dioxide accompanied by smoke is more fatal. They are injurious to plants also as they damage the leaf tissues.

Biochemical Effects of Ozone and PAN(peroxyacetvl nitrate): Being products of photochemical smog it is harmful to the plants, animals and human beings. It causes irritation of the eyes and respiratory tracts, causes pulmonary edema. In plants they are found to inhibit activity of enzymes which synthesize cellulose and lipids.

Biochemical Effects of Pesticides: DDT present in the pesticides affects the central nervous system. It is a persistent chemical. Once introduced into the environment it keeps circulating for years.

Occupational Hazards: In the long run, due to synergistic effect of various chemicals in the presence of excessive heat and lack of ventilation, and improper ergonomic condition, the major occupational health problems which can be expected are many. Common acute occupational illnesses observed are allergic skin diseases, allergic lung disorders, and irritation of eyes with lacrimation, photophobia and conjunctivitis. Long working hours, exposure to excessive heat, low illumination, improper posture, overcrowded working space, continuous sitting in one posture can cause health problems like pain in joints, bodyache, fatigue and other muscle skeletal problems, resulting in stunted physical growth and development. Over and above this many works induced psychological problems can't be ruled out.

Remedial Measures

***Waste Treatment Plants*:** Waste discharged from industries, agricultural lands, domestic areas etc. should be subjected to proper disposal. Waste treatment plants should be installed in industries. Recycling of waste should also be done in order to minimize environmental problems.

***Installation of Pollution Kits*:** Pollution kit should be installed in the vehicles to minimize pollution.

***Check on Population Growth*:** Population growth is a serious threat to the environment giving rise to a series of problems. Thus measures should be adopted to check the rapid growth of population.

***Public Awareness and Environmental Education Programme*:** A large part of the population in India is illiterate and lack environmental awareness. Environmental education should be introduced at the school level to make each and every one aware.

***Use of Non-toxic and Biodegradable Manures and Fertilizers*:** Manures produced from bio-gases and bio-degradable elements should be used to reduce the toxic effect.

***Conservation of Biodiversity*:** Loss of bio-diversity is a serious threat to mankind and environment. Conservation and protection of bio-diversity will help to solve many environmental problems.

***The Idea of Sustainability*:** The concept of sustainable development can lead us towards a strategy that will consider sustaining the environmental problems. The hopes of the developing nations and the needs of future generations as well.

11

Accumulation of Waste and Environmental Pollution

SADHANA SAXENA AND BINDU GANDHI

Environmental pollution is the undesirable change in physical, chemical and biological characteristics of air, water and soils. The chapter examines the role of such pollutants in environmental pollution.

It is generally known that an immeasurable quantity of pollutants is being continuously poured in the environment due to various kinds of human activities be they household, commercial or industrial. When these substances are not removed and get accumulated in large concentrations they pose serious health hazard and consequently become an ecological threat.

Pollutants of Environment

These pollutants can be classified as follows :

1. Solid waste pollutants
2. Liquid waste pollutants
3. Gaseous waste pollutants

Solid Waste Pollutants

Solid waste is generated in homes, offices, shops, institutions and industrial units. Pollution of environment due to improper management of solid waste is increasing day-by-day.

Common forms of solid waste pollutants are :

(a) Municipal Solid Waste (MSW)
(b) Bio-medical waste
(c) Agricultural waste
(d) Industrial waste
(e) Radioactive waste

These solid waste materials effect human health and environment in many ways. They spread cholera, typhoid, viral fever etc. and many other infectious diseases. Biodegradable and non-biodegradable agricultural waste when dumped near water body usually lead to water pollution. Poisonous gases cause air pollution, radioactive waste damages human cells and other animal cells. They also cause skin diseases and cancer.

Liquid Waste Pollutants

Waste material in the liquid form is a dangerous pollutant as it can flow easily, mix with water source and prove harmful for aquatic life as well as drinking water supply. Industrial effluents, discharge from household activities, sewage slurry from agricultural fields, waste water from paper mills, processing units, liquid waste from sugar mills, oil mills and some shampoos etc. are common forms of liquid pollutants that affect human life.

Gaseous Waste Pollutants

Gaseous waste products have three major sources that affect the environment. These are mainly dust, vehicular traffic, manufacturing units using any type of fuel, factories and a group of chemicals called chlorofluorocarbons. Vehicles and factories produce toxic gases such as carbon monoxide, carbon dioxide, sulphur dioxide and oxides of nitrogen and smoke etc.

Carbon monoxide is a poisonous gas as it combines with hemoglobin of our blood to make a stable compound called carboxyl—hemoglobin etc.

During respiration by human beings and animals and burning of fossil fuels etc., carbon dioxide is added to the atmosphere as a waste. Part of it is used by plants for photosynthesis, the rest remains in the atmosphere and causes air pollution. Carbon dioxide acts as a greenhouse gas. It has the property of absorbing the heat radiated by the earth, in the form of infrared rays. This heat is retained by CO_2 molecules and causes the temperature of earth to rise. The phenomenon is called 'Global Warning'. It results in the melting of ice caps and rise in the level of sea.

Oxides of sulphur and nitrogen undergo photochemical reactions, form acids and come drawn as 'acid rain'. Acid rain damages the crops and monuments. Smoke combines with fog to form a highly poisonous mixture called 'Smog' (Smoke + Fog = Smog). Smog and other toxic gaseous pollutants cause respiratory diseases, such as bronchitis and allergies. Chlorofluorocarbons (CFC's) are a group of chemicals used in refrigeration industry. Chlorofluorocarbons have been found to be responsible for depletion of ozone layer. Ozone layer protects us from harmful ultraviolet radiation of the sun. Depletion of ozone layer exposes the mankind to ultraviolet rays which cause skin cancer.

Besides CFC's, various kinds of sprays such as room-freshners, perfumes and deodorants, in fact, add poisonous chemicals to atmosphere instead of freshness.

12

Water Borne Pesticides and Related Health Impacts

SUNITA PHADNIS and REKHA KILLEDAR

Introduction

In the last few years research publications and magazines pointing out the nature and magnitude of the problem have extensively highlighted the presence of pesticides in ground and packaged water. Pesticides, herbicides and fungicides have been introduced during the mid-sixties on a large scale along with the other inputs for propogating the Green Revolution package in Indian agriculture. The main intention of the introduction of pesticides was to prevent and control insects and pests and diseases in field crops. Initially the use of pesticides reduced pest attack and paved the way for increasing the crop yield as expected. Simultaneously, increased use of chemical pesticides has resulted in contaminating the environment and long-term implications on the society are found to be many. Knowingly or unknowingly, now the farmers are addicted to using agro-chemicals indiscriminately and excessively, thus making the situation from bad to worse.

In India pesticide usage began in 1948 when DDT was imported for malaria control, whereas production started for hexa-chlorocyclohexane (HCH) in 1952. The present production of pesticides is 81,803 MT annually which is the largest in Asia and ranks 12th in the world.

In India pesticides are mainly being used to protect crops from insects and for public health purposes. The pesticides used for different purposes move between different environmental compartments and ultimately affect human beings. Pesticides that have been banned or restricted from use in many developed countries whereas countries like India have become dumping grounds for chemical pesticides.

One of the implications of pesticide use the extinction of useful organisms present in soil and/i.e., plants and animals like earthworms, bees, spiders, etc. The disposal of empty containers after pesticide application is one of the serious problems and has been responsible for pesticide contamination leading to chronic and acute problems to the exposed personnel.

Impact of Pesticide Uses

Pesticide Application

Insecticides contribute 75 per cent of the total pesticide consumption in the country and of that organochlorine and organophosphorous share 40 and 30 per cent respectively. In India pests cause crop loss of more than Rs. 6000 crores annually, of which 33 per cent is due to weeds, 26 per cent due to diseases, 20 per cent by insects, 10 per cent by birds and rodents and the remaining 11 per cent is due to other factors. Application of synthetic pesticides has increased significantly from 1950-51 to the late nineties related to the fact that the farmers are increasingly aware of the adverse effects of such inputs. Since, the last few years the focus on public policies towards pesticides has been changing more favourably for using biodegradable and environmentally sound pesticides like neemazol, repellin, wellgro, econeem and biopesticides.

Health Impact

Green vegetables have been detected with pesticide residues and their health impacts were reported in the State of Rajasthan.

Agricultural commodities like tea, egg powder and cashew kernels have been rejected on the contention of chemical contamination and presence of pesticide residue in European countries. A report from the largely chili producing State of Andhra Pradesh indicates that dry chilies too have pesticide particles and the importers refused to accept the consignment. Plantation Corporation of Kerala (PCK) reported that the continuous and indiscriminate application of pesticides on several cashew gardens in Padre village affected the flora and fauna and the local people became victims of severe problems like cancer.

Pesticide Spraying

The Indian Institute of Health Management in Jaipur, Rajasthan reported newborn children with Neutral Tube Defect (NTD), a deformity that results from the incomplete closure of neutral tube during early pregnancy and correlated with pesticides spraying. Alarming NTD takes a heavy toll of the order of half a million babies every year in the world and in Rajasthan alone around 8000 babies are reportedly affected. The study confirmed that the primary cause of NTD is the excessive use of pesticides on crop fields. Further, the study also notes that pesticides are mainly responsible for NTD as they are antagonistic to folic acid, a vitamin that essential for the development of the brain. Vegetables applied to the heavy dose of chemical pesticides and obviously the pregnant women, who eat such contaminated and toxic vegetables and green leafs succumbed to complications. The physician contends that pesticides residue in food can prevent the availability of folic acid leading to the birth of children with NTD.

In India, the reproductive performance of population exposed to pesticides in cotton fields was observed in 1991. In this 1016 couples were involved in which the males were not exposed to pesticides. Both these groups belonged to same social economic group and had same age range. Statistical analysis revealed a significant decrease of fertility in males and increased rate of abortions in females in pesticide-exposed group. This data was compared to the controlled group that was not exposed to pesticides.

Table 12.1: Health Disorders in Padre Village of Kerala

Disorders	*No.of Cases*
Cancer	49
Mental retardation	23
Congenital Anomalies	09
Psychiatric Cases	43
Epilepsy	23
Suicides	09
Total	156

Source : *Down to Earth* (2001)

Symptoms of Poisoning

The vulnerable groups of pesticides toxicity are agricultural labourers, marginal and small farmers and women labourers that succumb to pesticide related health disorders in the long run. The brief symptoms of pesticide poisoning are given in the Table 12.1.

Brief Symptoms of Pesticides Poison in India

Category	*System Affected*	*Common Symptoms*
Respiratory	Nose, Trachea, Lungs	Irritation, tight chest, coughing, chocking
Gastrointestinal	Stomach, Intestine	Nausea, vomitting, diarrhoea,
Renal	Kidney	back pain, urinating more or less than usual
Neurological	Brain, Spinal Cord	Headache dizziness, confusion, behaviour, depression, coma, convulsions
Hematological	Blood	Anemia (tiredness, weakness)
Dermatological	Skin, Eyes	Rashes, itching, redness, swelling
Reproductive	Ovaries, Testies, Fetus	Infertility, miscarriage

Source: Kamrin, 1997

Experimentation and Results

The pesticide analyses in water sample were carried out following the 18th edition of standard methods for the water and wastewater 1992. The standardization techniques optimized for the examination of contaminated water under Indian conditions were used.

The samples for experimentations were collected from tube wells, water tanks and some packaged drinking water for physico-chemicals studies. All the parameters were analysed in our laboratory except temperature, colour and pH which were noted at the sites. The analysis was based on studies like appearance, odour, temperature, pH, acidity, alkalinity, BOD, COD, pesticide present, presence of any metal or cyanide, chloride, phosphate, nitrate, oil and grease etc.

- Data indicated the contamination of water resources with pesticides.
- In packaged drinking water the levels were found not detectable except in two samples 0.131 ug/lt and 0.106 ug/lt DDT reported within the regulated WHO guideline values.

Alternatives to Synthetic Pesticides

The modern chemical farming has shifted slowly towards sustainable farming that depends on local farm resources across the world. Based on existing scenario and available inputs, if we consider the economic viability and environmental sustainability, certain alternatives can be given as following:

- Application of environmentally friendly plant based solutions.
- Ask the industries to spend more on labourers for developing alternatives which will increase the employment also.
- Private agencies should start preparation and supply of inputs like earthworms and plant based decoctions.

- Application of synthetic pesticide inputs must be a last option after every attempt.
- A strong political will to provide enough resources and above all stakeholder's full participation and co-operation.

Conclusion

All above study and discussion reveals that increased use of pesticides has caused economic, environmental, health and social problems. Lack of awareness among the farmers, deliberate suppression of facts, unlawful approaches, public policies and poor alternative mechanism is responsible for present scenario. Some actions for controlling or preventing pesticides impact on human health are suggested:

- Planning and implementing research on environmental protection from pesticides.
- Pesticide registration should be made very stringent.
- The pesticide industry which is the main polluter, should be taxed or should pay for developing decontamination techniques.
- Monitoring of pesticides in food items and drinking water should be done regularly.
- Tolerance limit for pesticides should be evaluated and made lower as compared to present limit.
- Studies, research and publication on hazardous effects of pesticides should be conducted to minimize the intake of pesticides.
- Organic farming and use of bio-pesticides like *neem* should be promoted.
- A national programme to create mass awareness should be launched and sustained.

Suggested Readings

(1) K.L. Saxena and T. Chakraborty, Organic pesticides and their removal from aqueous system 1978 *Indian Journal of Environmental Health,* October, 1978.

(2) M.K.K. Pillai, and H.C. Agrawal, DDT residues and its degradation in soil, water and a few aquatic animals of Jamuna I Delhi report submitted to the Department of Science and Technology, New Delhi 1979.
(3) Kruegar, R.F. and Seiber, J.D. (eds.), *Treatment and Disposal of pesticide water.* American Chemical Society Symposium Series No. 259 Washington DC. 1984.
(4) Oimenal, D.L., A. Mclaughlin, Environmental and Economic effects of reducing pesticide use. *Bioscience* 1991. 402-409.

13

Impact of Brick Industry on Soil Resources of Waghur River Basin

V.J.Patil, S.V. Dhake and R.V. Bhole

Introduction

The chapter attempts to examine the impact of brick making on soil fertility based on empirical evidences.

Study Area

Waghur river basin area near Sakegaon and Girna river basin area near Jalgaon have been selected for the purpose of present study. About 65 brick kiln units are located in this area.

Data Base and Methodology

The study is mainly based on primary sources of data which have been collected through questionnaire based on interviews and field surveys, i.e., survey of 13 units of brick kilns.

The field work was done in the years 2006. For getting accurate information the sampled brick kilns were visited frequently. The field study in this area had been conducted to understand the causes and effects of soil erosion.

Discussion

The study area is located in the northern part of the State of Maharashtra. Bhusawal and Jalgaon are the two urban centres adjacent to study area which require huge quantities of bricks for construction of physical structures for many purposes.

Location of Brick Kilns

Field surveys was conducted to locate the brick kilns lying in the basins of Waghur and Girna rivers. It was observed that the bricks are derived mostly from the nearby areas. Most of the brick kilns were located in the basin areas of Waghur and Girna rivers. There were 65 brick kilns in the study area. Availability of good quality soil, accessibility to the market and demand of bricks play an important role in the location of brick kilns.

Process of Manufacture of Bricks

For making of bricks good quality soil is required. In this region, all brick owners collect the soil from the following tahsils viz. Jalgaon, Bhusawal and Erandol tahsils. Mainly Black Cotton Soil is available in the study region. Some brick kiln owners get on lease the surrounding land for soil quarrying.

Soil quarrying removes about 5 to 6 feet of top fertile soil. So after 3 to 4 years the fertile agricultural land turns into a ditch, usually 5 feet deep.

Field surveys have also revealed that near about 1.5 hectares of land is required for location of one brick kiln. Farmers give their land on lease because of their monetary needs. But after the lease period is over the land becomes totally eroded, unleveled and polluted land. Field surveys revealed that about 300-400 hectares of land of study area were degraded, unleveled and un-reclaimed.

Presently 65 kilns are manufacturing bricks. The total brick production of study area per season is about 2 to 2.5 lakhs of bricks. One brick weighs 3 kg approximately. In this way, for producing 1000 bricks, three tonnes of soil is required. The total use of soil resources in study region is about 350 tonnes to 500 tonnes per season.

Ten soil samples were collected from the areas wherefrom soil is supplied to brick kiln both from un-quarried lands where agriculture is practiced and from quarried lands.

The sample were tested for their pH, organic matter, phosphorous and potash content.

Results of soil tests showed that there was 45.38 per cent decrease in organic matter, 60.20 per cent decrease in phosphorous and 28.32 per cent decrease in potash in the quarried lands.

It is also seen that the fertility of the quarried lands has gone down more.

Conclusion

All brick manufacturing activities use large amount of soil. About 350 to 500 tonnes of soil per year is eroded in the brick manufacturing activities in Waghur and Girnar rivers basin area. All soil is collected from the agricultural land so there is a loss of good agricultural soil.

REFERENCES

Asgher, S.M. (2002): "Impact of Brick kilns on land and Environment in and around Aligarh City" Unpublished Ph. D Thesis A.M.U. Aligarh.

Kadam, Anuradha, Saptarshi Pravin and Kadam Avinash : " Impact of Brick Industry on physical environment", Research paper published in *Maharashtra Bhugolshashtra Patrika,* Vol XVI N: 2, July-Dec. 2002.

14

Double Green Revolution and Quality of Environment
An Overview

MANISHA DANDAWATE

It is widely known that green revolution changed the picture of Indian agriculture vis-à-vis its economy. Green revolution lead farmers to use hybrid varieties of seeds, chemical fertilizers to enhance production, chemical pesticides to control pests, feticides to control weeds and employ better irrigation facilities. All these practices increased agri-production manyfold. The success of green revolution made farmers greedy. On one hand Indian farmers earned more money but on the other hand increased soil erosion, salinization, scarcity of water and air pollution, etc. After 50 years of green revolution now the side effects of green revolutions are becoming clear.

"Green revolution became greed revolution" because of many reasons. Farmer was not aware what exact amount of chemicals he should use to have sufficient production and for pest control, etc. The chemicals which he used like DDT, BHC, Gamaxine, Alderin, etc. not only spoiled the soils but harmed flora and fauna of adjacent water bodies also. The residues or traces of these elements are reaching into food-stuffs (like in vegetables, fruits, eggs, chicken and milk, etc.) leading to various health hazards. They are disturbing human systems such as respiratory, reproductory, dermal, etc. The traces of chemicals (leftovers on vegetables and fruits etc.) found on food-stuffs sometimes cause abortions. DDT, BHC is already banned in many countries. When these chemicals reach into water bodies they kill fish and other life forms. This may disrupt the food chain, ecological balance, purity of water and so on.

In order to overcome the side effects of green revolution or 'greed revolution' scientists are stepping forward towards "double green revolution" and "gene revolution". Today scientists can introduce any gene from any organism to another, like a gene can be isolated from bacteria and can be introduced into any plant, animal or virus like the variety of cotton, i.e. Bt. Cotton. A gene is isolated from bacteria and introduce into cotton. Now Bt. Cotton is successful for some regions but a failure in others.

In spite of the agri-revolution the farmer is not getting his cost of production. The issue of farmers committing suicides in many areas in Maharashtra and other states of the country is being debated in context of green revolution and its impact on agriculture in general. The farmer is purchasing hybrid and genetically engineered seeds, using many chemical fertilizers, pesticides, etc. A lot of money is invested in irrigation facilities. Still the farmer is not getting proper production. Sometimes to fulfill all needs the farmer takes loan from bank but because of less production he fails to return it and becomes bankrupt and ultimately commits suicide.

To overcome all these problems there is organic farming which is non-violent farming or evergreen farming. It is a cheaper method of cultivation as well as it is eco-friendly. In organic farming chemical fertilizer are replaced by bio-fertilizers. The fertilizers are made from organic wastes like waste leaves, vegetable waste, food residue, cow dung, etc. for this vermin-composting method is very useful. The method is cheap as well as all organic waste material can be utilised. By using vermin-compost the fertility of soil increases. Further, in organic farming instead of chemicals pesticides and feticides bio-pesticides are used. These work on biological control system like pheromone trap are used. This trap contains a substance which has a specific smell resembling female hormone. Now when this trap in "on" it spreads specific smell that works on biological control system, which attracts all male insects and they are trapped in this. Leguminous corps increase the fertility of the soils. All these methods are eco-friendly and cheap also. The advanced technology is always welcome but it should be suitable for Indian circumstances. In fact any new variety of seed or crop needs 15 years minimum time for trail. But today everyone wants fast results. So scientists should first think of Indian circumstances, and should guide farmers in that direction so that farmer will benefit from their research. Indian scientists must accept the challenge of organic revolution. It is the need of our environment and future generations.The best efforts to achieve maximum production is through organic revolution. A dream and vision given by Dr. A.P.J. Abdul Kalam will become true and fruitful that the research of scientist should reach and benefit to common one.

15

Nuclear Energy
A Source of Radioactive Pollution

S. Bhatt

Introduction

The chapter deals with various aspects of radioactive pollution, its impact on mankind, causes and ways of minimizing the threat so arising.

Energy released from the atomic nucleus is known as nuclear energy. It follows the conversion of its mass to energy consistent with Einstein's formula $E=mc_2$ in which E = Energy, M= Mass, and C = the speed of light.

Nuclear energy is released by one of three nuclear reactions:

- Fission, heavy nucleus is split into two light nuclei nearly of the same size. Fission reactions are widely used for production of nuclear energy (nuclear power plant, nuclear weapons, etc).
- Fusion, the fusing together of atomic nuclei.
- Decay, is a term used for the slower natural fission process of a nucleus breaking down into a more stable form.

The 1940's was the nuclear era where the first nuclear bomb was being developed. Nuclear era reached its greatest peak in the world war, by showing its massive ability of destroying things. Nuclear energy has been recognized as a clean energy because it doesn't release pollutants such as CO_2 to the atmosphere after its reaction that could damage our environment. It is also known that nuclear energy has reduced the amount of greenhouse gas emission, reducing emissions of CO_2. Despite the advantage of nuclear energy as a clean energy, the big concern is the waste resulting from nuclear reaction, which is a form of pollution, called radioactivity. It is a form of radiation.

There are commonly three types of radiation, namely:

- Alpha rays, can be blocked by a piece of paper and human skin.
- Beta rays, can be blocked by some pieces of glass and metal, and can penetrate through skin.
- Gamma rays, can only be blocked by a very thick, strong, massive piece of concrete, and can penetrate easily to human skin and damage cells on its way through.

Radioactive Pollution

Radioactive pollution is the release of radioactive substances or high-energy particles into the air, water, or earth as a result of human activity, either by design or by accident. Since even a small amount of radiation exposure can have serious and cumulative biological consequences, and since many radioactive wastes remain toxic for centuries, radioactive pollution is a serious environmental concern.

The difficulty in assessment of the effects of radioactive pollution makes it a bigger problem. Radioactive waste may spread over a broad area quite rapidly and irregularly and may not fully show its effects upon humans and organisms. Radioactive materials are under the jurisdiction of governmental agencies (usually in the secretive defense and military establishments). The dumping activities and accidental discharges that accompany nuclear materials production and bomb testing tend to remain concealed until governments disclose them under public pressure.

Sources of Radioactive Pollution

One can classify major sources that lead to radioactive pollution to the following categories:

Nuclear power plants

- The waste resulted, in form of radioactivity, brings hazard when unsafely maintained.
- Nuclear power plant accidents will endanger the life and surrounding environment.

Nuclear weapon

- Nuclear weapon tests that are conducted above groundwater or underwater.
- Nuclear bombing such as what have happened in Hiroshima and Nagasaki will create devastation in a short time.

Transportation

- Transportation (air, land, water, sea) of nuclear wastes from one place to another will bring serious hazards to the environment if they are not maintained carefully and/or facing accidents.

Disposal of nuclear waste

- The decaying process of radioactive wastes takes a very long time in progress. Some radioactive substances have long half-life are dangerous in that great amount of period. A half-life is the period of time required for the disintegration of half of the atoms in a sample of a radioactive substance. There are common ways to dispose nuclear waste: burying under ground very deeply and burying under the sea. However, they are still dangerous and expensive. Science is still on its way finding a better way to solve this problem.

Uranium Mining

- Uranium, substance that is used in nuclear power plants, is harvested from uranium mining. Uranium mining results in radioactive waste that pollutes the surrounding environment.

Radioactive Material

Following radioactive materials are used in generation of nuclear energy:

- *Uranium (U)*—Uranium which is used as a fuel in nuclear reactors and nuclear bombs causes lung cancer, tumors of the lymphatic and non-malignant respiratory disease.
- *Plutonium (Pu)*—Plutonium, an artificially created radioactive material is used in bombs and reactors, has carcinogenic effects which promote cancer development, mutation to body tissues and cells and disruption to normal fetal development.
- *Lead (Pb)*—Lead is used as a protective shield from radioactivity in nuclear reactors causes mental retardation among children exposed to lead in water resulting from lead pipes and solders in older water systems and leads to weakness, general disability, nervous disorders and eventual death.
- *Cadmium (Cd)*—Cadmium which is used as nuclear reactor regulator is toxic and poisonous.

Types of Radioactive Pollution

Atmospheric Pollution

Radioactive pollution that is spread through the earth's atmosphere is termed *fallout*. There are three types of fallout resulting from nuclear detonations:

- *Local Fallout*: This fallout is quite intense but short-lived.
- *Tropospheric Fallout*: This fallout (in the lower atmosphere) is deposited at a later time and covers a larger area, depending on meteorological conditions.
- *Stratospheric Fallout*: This fallout, which releases extremely fine particles into the upper atmosphere, may continue for years after an explosion and attain a worldwide distribution.

The two best known examples illustrating the effect of fallout contamination are the bombing of Hiroshima and Nagasaki, Japan in 1945 and the Chernobyl Nuclear Power Station disaster in April 1986.

Pollution on Land and Water

The major sources of radioactive pollution on land and water include:

(1) *The nuclear fuel cycle*—The extraction, separation and refinement of materials for use in nuclear weapons and nuclear power, and
(2) *The day-to-day operations of nuclear power plants*—For spent nuclear fuel from these plants, a high-level waste, no completely reliable disposal method exists. Most low-level waste (anything that is not spent fuel or transuranic waste) generated by nuclear power plants has been land filled.

Nuclear Minerals and Human Activities

The nuclear chain consists of human activities that begin with disturbing natural radioactive uranium deep in the earth, and includes every stage of mining, milling, transporting, enriching, fabricating, processing, and so-called disposal. Every link in this chain results in contamination of the biosphere. As wind and water, microbes, insects, seeds, birds, and other life forms move through all ecosystems, unconfined radioactivity eventually disperses through the biosphere worldwide. Contamination continues at every step along the way without end in the reactors, the submarines, the weapons manufacturing, stockpiling, storage, testing, use, and dismantlement. Whether through misplaced priorities, by plan or by accident, the development of nuclear technology has been accompanied by gross as well as minute releases of radioactivity into the atmosphere, the soils, the oceans, seas, and water table, showing up worldwide in animal, vegetable, and inert matter. Radiation crosses species and concentrates through the food chain, subjecting other animals and humans to its damaging effects.

Effects of Radioactive Pollution

As even a small amount of radiation exposure can have serious biological consequences and since much radioactive waste remain for centuries, radioactive pollution is a serious environmental concern.

Biomedical Effects

The greatest threat of radioactivity to life is damage to the gene pool, the genetic make-up of all living species, which is cumulative over lifetimes and generations. Some biomedical effects of radiation are well known. Even low-dose exposures are carcinogenic after extended exposure. The current generation, the one in utero, and all that follow may suffer cancers, immune system damage, leukemia's, stillbirths, deformities, and fertility problems. The quality of lives of countless people have been affected by radiation exposure.

Psychological Damage

Knowing that, because of the presence of nuclear materials, our planet, our home, our selves could be irreparably destroyed at any moment, impairs our ability to engage in meaningful, successful, protective strategies. Beyond the physiological effects, the mental and emotional consequences of the trauma of exposure to invisible environmental contaminants in general, and radioactivity in particular, has been documented.

Prevention and Minimisation

For overcoming radioactive pollution and to preserve the environment there is a need for following actions:

Research and Developments

- *Management of buried waste and contaminated soil*: This can be done either by leaving buried waste in place with constant observations and monitoring and also by upgrading and improvisation of containment or by removing, processing and disposing of waste in repository.
- *Storage*: Waste is offloaded from local collection routes and sorted according to types. The separated wastes are then loaded onto larger vehicles for transportation to either a municipal waste treatment or disposal facility.
- *Construction of thick earthen cover* (Uranium Mill Tailings) at the site of mining: protection by rock to avoid leeching/seepage into groundwater over waste, balance and stabilize piles of rock covers to avoid dispersion of tailings through erosion or intrusion which can be transferred to safer location and efficiently control radon emission and gamma radiation.

- *Monitored Retrievable Storage (MRS) facility*: Receive and store spent fuel from commercial power reactors for subsequent shipment to a repository.
- *Solid waste Treatment*: The volume of accumulated solid waste is decreased by combustion and the remains of ashes are coordinated in its management to prevent detrimental and catastrophic effects to environment.

Disposal

Mined Geologic Repositories

Spent fuel and high level radioactive waste may be disposed off in mined geologic repositories. The site for the repositories is evaluated and geological, hydrological and geochemical conditions are studied and designed for matching the requirements of NRC.

Land filling

It consists of liner system and leach at collection systems to avoid contamination of groundwater under landfill and impermeable cover is laid over landfill when the site cease operation to prevent rainwater from entering.

Injection Wells

These are used in disposal of liquid waste injected under high pressure thousands of feet underground. These are designed and operated to avoid leakage of waste (underground confinement waste).

Laws and Regulations

Enforcement of law to ensure smooth implementation and to act as deterrent to others against the unscrupulous offenders committing such offences to bring them to justice. Governments at any level must manage the preservation of environment by enforcing laws and regulations.

Human Activities

Government and Non-Governmental Organizations (NGOs) encourage public participation on the sustainable management of environment, and as a medium of communications between the public and government concerning environmental issues. Cooperation and partnerships between international communities must be developed to reach a mutual objective in prevention of pollution and conservation of environment worldwide.

Protocols and Conventions

Implementations and adoption of protocols discussed and exchange ideas and opinions by scientist, environmentalist and leaders worldwide on the measures on prevention, treatments and control, and management on the global environmental state facing every nations.

Education

Imparting knowledge and value of significance of the environment to gain every individual sense and consciousness the wealth of biodiversity and ecology.

Environmental Ethics

Mankind is not everything, we are part of nature and it is provided for all living things. We must execute the responsibility to care for nature's continual conservation, stability and beauty and play a good and honest role as a part of nature to maintain environmental equilibrium. The use of natural resources must be as efficient as possible since natural resources are limited, we have to preserve and save it for the future.

Conclusion

All human accomplishments will amount to nothing if future generations are sickened, crippled, and killed on a massive scale by the toxic by-products of nuclear energy. Radioactive pollution constitutes one of the most menacing threats to the present and future of humankind, because of its endurance over time and its ubiquity and invisibility.

Citizen groups and government and non-governmental organizations around the world have begun to address radioactive pollution.

A comprehensive global approach must be developed to manage all radioactive materials over the generations that they will exist. Political, military, and business leaders and ordinary citizens must face the problem together.

SECTION-C

TECHNO-POLITICAL RESPONSES

16

Application of Remote Sensing in Environmental Planning

NARESH KUMAR and ANJULA POIUS

Introduction

The chapter underlines that remote sensing as a tool can provide information beyond the visible spectrum and in that respect it may add to environmental planning in a more effective manner. The paper highlights definitional aspects of the theme and then demonstrates various elements of environment in the planning of which remote sensing can play an effective role.

The term "Environment" embraces all physical aspects which embrace the earth including resources. It is a known fact that in the long process of un-planned utilization of resources the ecological balance has been upset. Environmental planning is the need of the hour. It requires the establishment of a system to ensure that societal activities are carried on in a way that permits the maintenance of a healthy and productive habitat.

Planning is a continuous process of decision-making irrespective of whether it is a long-term or a short-term planning. For efficient planning one needs accurate, reliable and timely information. The information mix must have basic data on static and dynamic aspects. A proper information system and its constant updating is also a necessity at all levels of planning. In this context remote sensing can play a very important role as it provides reliable and updated information of natural resources and environment.

Remote Sensing

Remote sensing is the acquisition of physical information from a source that is stationed in a remote location. In other words remote sensing is a means to get reliable information without being in physical contact with the object concerned. It is based on the observation of an object by a device separated from it by some distance, utilizing the characteristic response of different objects to emissions in the electromagnetic spectrum, due to their differing reflectance and emissive. This electromagnetic energy is measured in a number of spectral bands for the purpose of identification of the object. This measurement (data collection) is made with the help of sensors that detect the radiation from different object. Satellite platforms allow large area coverage at frequent intervals and are highly suited for application based on synoptic measurements. The integration of remote sensing with the conventional system of mapping and monitoring provides accurate and reliable information in a timely and cost effective manner. Regular monitoring is needed to take stock of environmental balance such as depletion of forest cover, degradation of land, water resources etc. Such information is very essential for proper environmental planning.

Environmental Planning

Planning activities are generally concerned with the objectives of preserving or enhancing environmental values or resources. All planning is based on what is available on the earth. The process of planning consists of an applied appraisal of the present situation, its positive and negative features and their prospects. A brief account of factors responsible for the present situation and to develop assumptions for the future in consideration of alternative courses of action available for selection against the conflicting interests should precede planning. There is another word which is very much in use these days. It is environmental management which may follow planning steps for maintaining the efficiency of the planned system.

Improving the quality of the citizens is the main policy objective of socio-economic development in all countries of the world. However, in order to ensure that human activities interfere only to an acceptable degree with the functioning of life support system or natural ecological process, environmental planning is now becoming increasingly important.

Application of Remote Sensing in Environmental Planning

There are certain invisible aspects of the environment on the basis of which one can say that remote sensing plays a vital role in environmental planning. These may be summarized as under:

(a) A capacity for recording more permanently the patterns which are detected. This permits a more free inspection of the features of special interest.
(b) A broader and more selective ability to detect variation in environmental conditions.
(c) A better recall system, so that the pattern at different points in time might be compared with greater accuracy.
(d) Means of enhancing images, to reveal or highlight the selective phenomena.
(e) The traditional techniques of mapping of existing natural resources can be complemented with satellite remote sensing techniques .

A few examples may be cited as under—

Land Use

Proper utilization of land is essential in order to create a healthy environment. The satellite imagery provides a land use planner with a new source of data. This data can be used in the context of increasing population pressure on the available land. This new technique can generate the patterns of land utilization for different purposes that is for lifestyle, forestry, agriculture, industry, etc. and the present and the future need of land may be planned.

Hydrology

Remote sensing techniques are applicable to many areas of hydrology, including groundwater, surface water, snow and ice studies. The landsat imageries facilitate surface water mapping, flood plain mapping, tracing of river beds which is useful for ground and river drainage and command area studies, water quality, snow mapping, including the snow line and water pollution, etc. The effluence of commercial and industrial activity often contrast sharply with the water which receive them, satellite imageries have been used in many instances to identify and map the discharge patterns from sewage outlets and industrial complexes.

Soils

Association of the soils, identification and mapping have been accomplished using satellite data. Saline, alkaline and ravine areas can be identified and delineated. The imagery also aids in the study and preservation of soil erosion.

Bio-Vegetation

Remote sensing technique is useful in the field of vegetation studies, including agriculture, assessments of damage from insect, infestations and fires, harvest prediction, bio-analysis and wet land mapping.

Geology

The large area coverage from satellite platforms has proved to be extremely valuable in geological mapping. Detection and mapping of large lineaments, faults and fracture is possible from satellite data. The greatest contribution of the satellite data for geological studies has been in the field of structural analysis.

Pollution

Remote sensing technology provides valuable information on the quality of environmental system. Detection, measurement and monitoring of the environmental pollution with the help of satellite techniques is now in use.

Weather satellites provide accurate regular and long-term weather data which is required to know trends of temperature, rainfall, etc. Early warning of the danger of floods, droughts, landslides, glacier movement, cyclones etc. is possible.

Conclusion

From the above discussion it can be concluded that the remote sensing tool can be applied in environmental planning. The importance of remote sensing is now being recognized in the commercial sectors by environmental scientists. A comprehensive long-term remote sensing programme can be organized to establish meteorological base lines and determine how projected atmospheric conditions will affect air quality in areas likely to be affected by industrial or other atmospheric effluents.

An analysis of images employing multispectral processing with computer compatible digital tapes can clearly reveal different classes of sedimentation. The high sedimentation is caused by sand and gravel operations and run-off from construction sites. Organic pollution also can be identified as evident from major sewage outfalls in the estuary.

Remote sensing is undoubtedly the most accurate, reliable and near real time geographic tool. It extends geographers' capabilities of observation over the space and time and beyond visible portion of electromagnetic spectrum and provides repetitive observations of the phenomena of geographic interests.

17

Wealth from Waste

Archana Kanthed

Introduction

For stable economic development resources must be used carefully and technologies for recycling of wastes are to be evolved. The choice is between one time use of materials, i.e. throwaway society, and use of recycled materials, i.e. sustainable society. The chapter discusses recycling techniques and how best they can be used for making wealth from waste materials on one hand and can help in maintaining the quality of the environment.

Recycling Techniques

1. Crushing of materials as discarded household materials and appliances, etc.
2. Selection for magnetic, non-magnetic and specific gravity based materials.
3. Thermal decomposition of organic waste in the form of gas and oil.
4. Food sources from organic wastes for livestock.
5. Melting plastic, domestic toys and molding into new ones.
6. Melting blast furnace slag for making artificial jewellery etc.

7. Recycling of paper, plastic, petroleum products and chemicals.
8. Prevention of secondary pollution.

Construction Materials from Wastes

1. Water works silt.
2. Waste from sugar factories.
3. Agricultural wastes.
4. Coconut and cashewnut waste after oil extraction.
5. Utilizing fly ash.

Utilizing Agricultural Waste

It is known that agricultural waste like crushed sugarcane, bagasse, etc. are chief sources of cellulose. But it is burnt away as a cheap fuel. For a better economy, it is an essential step to get some by-products like protein from waste materials, which will not only solve the protein deficiency problem, but also reduce the amount of wastes, agricultural waste, e.g. papaya stem, wheat and paddy husk, *jowar* chaff, cotton stalk etc. are used in paper making.

Medicines from Agricultural Wastes

Furan compounds occur widely in nature and are cheap raw materials. Furfural is readily obtainable from agricultural wastes such as corn cobs and oat hulls. Furfural is the basic material used for the synthesis of nitro furans. These are important germicides used for treating cattle diseases. Nitro furazone or furacin are now being used for treatment of eyes, ears, sinus diseases, vaginal infections and post surgery skin infections. Nitrofurans are widely used in treating poultry diseases.

Liquid Fuels from Agricultural Waste

Recent studies shows that agricultural wastes have the potential to become a major source of liquid fuels and cellulose fibers. Central straws contain 45 per cent Cellulose 35 per cent hemicellulose and 10 per cent lignin. Cellulose is used for paper-making.

Proteins from Cellulose Waste

Experiments carried out at L. S. University, USA have shown the possibility of commercializing a process for making proteins from waste cellulose.

Cellulose Wastes into Sugars—A New Method

Agricultural cellulose wastes such as bagasse, corncobs and alfalfa etc. can be converted into glucose by a new technique.

Utilization of Cellulose Waste by Bacteria

Recent studies shows that bacteria can convert cellulose into about 55 per cent protein and amino acid.

Attention may now be paid to the efforts that have been made in the country in this respect.

Efforts in India

For an efficient disposal of solid cellulose waste in metropolitan cities to control soil pollution problems, Cotton Technology Research Laboratory (CTRL), Bombay, have developed a programme for large scale production of cellulose from *Pencillium funiculosum.*

Urban Waste and Bagasse for Electricity

Recent research in Indonesia has shown that urban wastes and bagasse from sugarcane can be used to generate electricity.

Agricultural Waste into Cheap and Efficient Fuel

Indian scientists, have developed a technology of converting agricultural wastes like rice husk and groundnut shells into briquetters to be used as an efficient, economical and not polluting fuel.

Bio Mass into Rural Power

All energy requirements of a village can be met locally from the available bio-mass, using Fluidised Bed Technology (FBT), which is a cheap and effective technique for combustion.

Ashes to Assets

After threshing, rice husk is generally used for burning purposes. But scientists at Shriram Institute (Delhi) have extracted an industrially useful project from the ashes of rice husk. They converted the waste into an extremely pure form of silica, which has now been used in rubber, plastic and paint industries.

Rubber from Old Tyres

A waste recycling plant in Germany has developed a technology of converting plastic wastes into oil.

Cash from Trash

Tata Chemicals is recovering valuable chemicals such as magnesium, soda ash and calcium carbonate, etc. from effluents discharged at various plants in India.

Energy from Wastes

The Ministry of Non-Conventional Energy Sources (MNES) has recently started a $ 5.5 million project funded by the Global Environment facility to convert municipal and industrial waste into energy.

Taking the Dirt Out of Plastic

Plastics are non-bio degradable substances that pile up in landfills. In plastic making hazardous substances and chemicals are used. These substances end up as large quantities of pollutants and toxic wastes. North Carolina University have taken the lead with a new method that obviates the need for harmful solvents.

Garbage to Gold (Fuel Pallets and Bio Fertilizers)

Everyday, the 10 million Bombayites throw out more than 4,000 tonnes of garbage. The Department of Science and Technology (DST) has set up a plant to convert organic waste into fuel pellets for industries. Excel Industries Ltd. have set up two plants to make compost from garbage. The compost so formed is a bioorganic soil enricher, which is capable of increasing the fertilizer efficiency and soil fertility.

Silk Industry Waste as Poultry Feed

According to researchers of the Cotton College, Guwahati, the silk industry wastes containing large quantities of waste pupae can be used as poultry feed.

Fly Ash into Bricks and Cement

Fly ash a waste material of coal fired thermal power stations, has been utilized as building bricks and cement.

Conclusion

In India the re-use of waste materials i.e. recycling would not only solve the problem of waste disposal but also the problem of rural unemployment.

18

Planning and Management of Environment
A Collaborative Model

RASHMI GUPTA

Introduction

Human beings have progressively made greater demands on environmental resources through an unprecedented increase in technological capacity, energy consumption, international trade, and social complexity. Environmental management can provide a way out to balance the man-environment interface in order to sustain life on the earth. This chapter explores the applicability of system modelling technique to environmental management.

Systems Modelling

This goal, however, involves several challenges. Applicability of modelling techniques to environmental management is affected by many factors. First of all, environmental systems are complicated, where some factors and interrelationships are hard to be expressed as mathematical formulas. For example, non-linearity that exists in a system can hardly be effectively reflected. Secondly, information about some system parameters is often unavailable, such that rough estimations have to be made. Also, a large portion of available information may not be quantifiable.

This type of information could simply be the implicit knowledge from decision-makers. Thus, the input into a modelling system may only be a small part of the entire information in a study system. Consequently, the modelling output is inadequate to support decision-making. The remaining part of the work should be a solid investigation on ambiguous and un-quantifiable information using innovative information technologies. Thirdly, a significant part of quantifiable information may not exist as deterministic data. This brings about the difficulty in uncertainty expression, as well as solving the models that contain uncertain parameters and/or relationships.

An associated challenge is to develop the capability of minimizing the uncertainties and risks using advanced information technologies. To overcome the challenges and to enhance model feasibility and applicability, there is a need for incorporating current information processing techniques.

Environmental management systems generally have multi-objective, interactive, dynamic and uncertain features. Complexities have to be tackled in determination of system parameters, reflection of interactive relationships, formulation of modelling approaches, interpretation of research outputs, and implementation of recommended policies. Often, to quantify such systems, simplifications have to be made, such as linear, continuous, static, single-objective, and/or deterministic assumptions.

These simplifications, however, would be responsible for the final errors which do occur. How to effectively reflect these complexities when bearing with these involved risks has been a challenging issue facing environmental researchers.

Many challenges exist in the applications of modelling techniques to environmental management. Most environmental models can only deal with limited spatial and temporal units in a system due to difficulties in computational requirement and data availability. The collection of environmental statistics is fraught with difficulties, due to wide range of environmental phenomena, data sources, and agencies involved, as well as the complexities of their temporal and spatial characteristics. Consequently, many environmental data are subject to serious discretion in regards to uncertainties, inconsistencies, and errors. In order to obtain improved reliability and certainty, solid works on validation of input-data prior to being used for further analysis are desired, where information technology could play crucial role.

Multi-stakeholder collaboration can act as a transformative mechanism for enabling communities and associated stakeholders to constructively address complex and long-standing issues concerning environmental and public health hazards, strained or non-existent relations with government agencies and other institutions, and economic decline. Multi-stakeholder collaboration in the environmental justice context can be transformative in two ways. First, it can provide disadvantaged communities with an opportunity to openly discuss concerns and potential solutions to issues affecting them in a manner that genuinely suits the affected community's needs. Second, it can provide public service organizations, including government agencies and community-based organizations, with an effective forum to coordinate, leverage, and strategically use resources to meet complex public health, environmental, and other socio-economic challenges facing disadvantaged communities.

Much of the success of these efforts can be attributed to individuals, either at the community, regional, NGO, or government level, who took it upon themselves, at real risk of failure, to pull diverse groups together. Pulling partnerships together, especially when the goal is to address challenging environmental problems and social relationships, and/or help a community revitalize, can be a difficult endeavour. This challenge is magnified when organizations are not accustomed to working in a coordinated manner, and when resources for maintaining the partnerships are not always readily available. Such an effort requires not only leadership skills, patience, and the ability for creative thinking, but also strong interpersonal skills that naturally lend themselves to stakeholder bridge building. In many instances, such a combination of skills in one individual may not be available; nevertheless it confirms the need for communities and other institutions desiring to use collaborative partnerships to look for these qualities in persons to lead or co-lead these efforts.

Conclusion

This evaluation examined the value of using collaborative partnerships to address environmental justice issues in predominantly low-income or down trodden communities. Quantitative environmental models have been challenged by the difficulties in handling dynamic and uncertain features of real-world environmental systems. Conditions for environmental management will keep changing with time, demanding periodically updated decision support. It is thus desired by users and decision-makers that the research outputs be dynamic. Advance in information technology has been in a extraordinarily rapid pace. There will be continuous attempts to apply new techniques and tools to environmental management.

SECTION-D

FOCUS ON INDORE CITY AND ITS ENVIRONMENT

19

Quality of Groundwater in Indore City
A Spatial Analysis

VENU TRIVEDI and BHAKTI CHOUREY

Water is the elixir of life. It is the principal component of the existence of human society. The chapter attempts a spatial analysis of quality of groundwater of Indore city.

Study Area

Indore, a fast growing commercial capital of Madhya Pradesh, has not escaped from the burning problem of scarcity of potable water. Indore city is situated on Malwa Plateau (23°46′ N latitude and 76°42′ E longitude) with an attitude of 550 metres above MSL (Fig. 19.1). Indore is one of the important and most populated city of the State having 15.97 lac population in 2001.

Aims and Objectives

The main objectives of the present study are as follows :

- To know the spatial distribution of groundwater quality on the basis of parameter taken for the analysis.
- To assess the causes responsible for poor groundwater quality.
- To suggest remedial actions to control the problem.

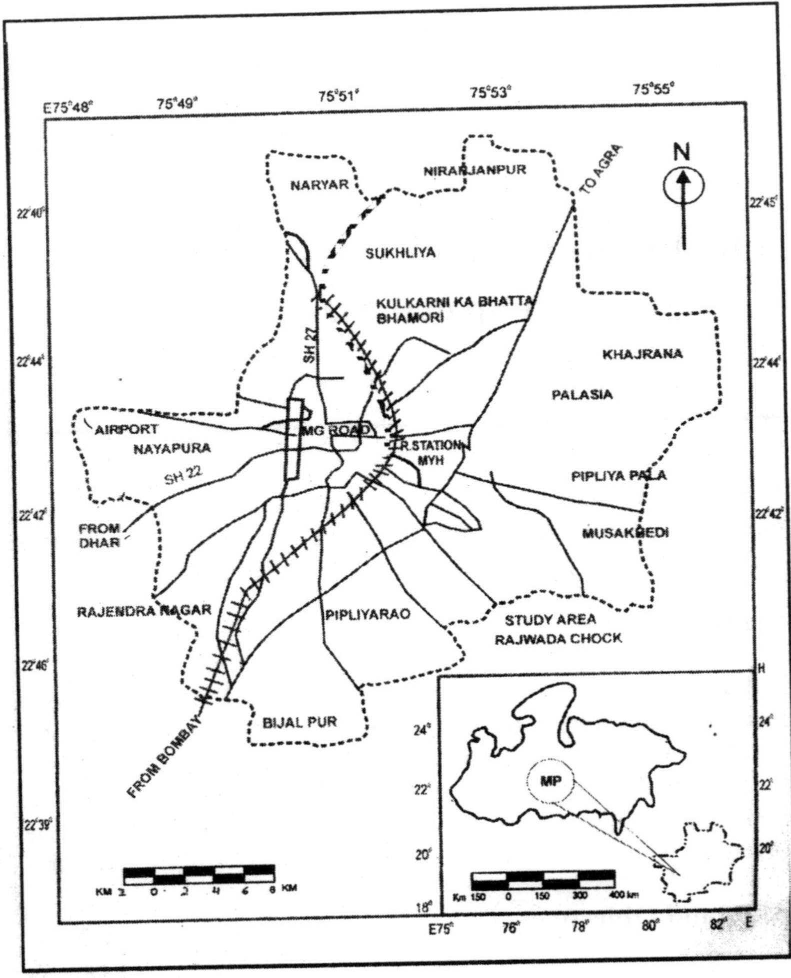

Fig. 19.1: Indore City : Base Map

Database and Methodology

The present study is based upon the primary source of information and experiments. Assessment of quality of ground-water in four different areas of Indore city, i.e. Industrial,

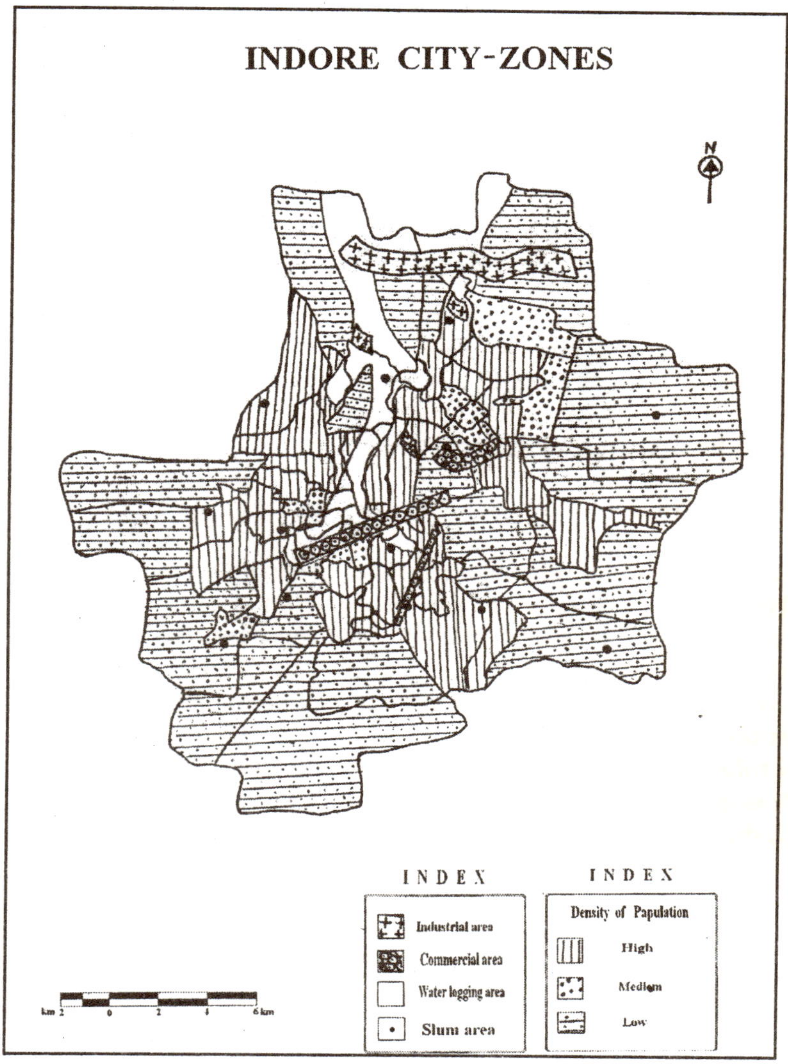

Fig. 19.2: Indore City Zones

Commercial, Residential and Slums has been made (Fig. 19.2). The quality of water is assessed on the basis of parameters of drinking water e.g. temptation, pH, turbidity, flouride, chloride, nitrate, iron, hardness, ammonia and faecal matter. A sample survey has been done in year 2006-07.

Discussion

Since Indore city is expanding at a galloping speed the deficit in supply and actual demand of water is generally met from pumping of groundwater through tubewells. With an increase in population, the number of tubewells is also increasing geometrically, resulting in over exploitation of groundwater. Continuous decrease of groundwater table in Indore is a matter of great concern, drying of tubewells in summer season being observed even at a depth of 100-150 meters.

The study of selected parameters in four different areas of Indore city is as follows.

Temperature

Direct sun light is the major cause for rise in water temperature. Therefore, warmer water can be expected in summer during the day time. It is important to take temperature reading at the same time of the day, if readings have to be compared. From the academic point of view it may be mentioned that for potable water, temperature of about 10°C is highly desirable, while temperature of about 25°C are considered objectionable. It is quite evident from Table 19.1 that in some part e.g. Juna Rishla (26°C), Katkatpura (26°C) residential access and highly commercialised M.G.Road (31°C), Jawahar Marg (26°C), Malharganj (26°C), Cloth Market (27°C) and Chhawani (26°C) the temperature is objectionable.

In Sanwer Road B and F sector and in slum area, except Lala ka Bagicha, the temperature is objectionable.

pH (potentia hidrogenji Hydrogen ion concentration)

pH value gives an idea of the intensity of the acidic or basic nature of a water sample. pH scale for aqueous solutions lies between 0-14, higher concentration of hydrogen ions gives lower score on the pH scale, while lower concentration of hydrogen ions gives higher score on the pH scale. As the pH value extends farther from pH 7 the acidity or alkalinity increases. The increase are not indirect pH scale.

pH Scale

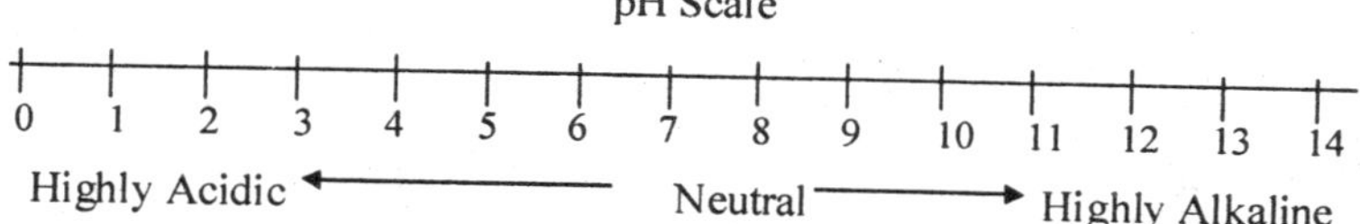

Proportion to the pH but are loganithmic function of the values.

Groundwater absorbs minerals present in the soil and acquires their characteristics. If the soil contains salt deposits, the water becomes alkaline. In the present study (Table 19.1), it is seen that pH value of Katkatpura residential area, M.G. Road commercial area, Sanwer Road, A, B and H sector industrial area, and in Pancham ki Phel slum area is increasing. It shows that alkalinity is 10 times higher than the permissible limit.

Turbidity

Turbidity in water is caused by the substances not present in the form of true solution. True solution have a practical size of less than 10^{-9}m. Any surface having more than this size will produce a turbidity. Turbidity is the result of fine solids in water. These solids can be in the form of silt, clay, saul industrial wastes, sewage, organic matter, phytoplantation and other microscopic organics. Turbidity makes water fit for domestic and industrial purposes. In drinking water the permissible limit is 5-10 ntu (nephelometric turbidity unit, nephelometer is known as turbidity meter). Table 19.1 shows that in Katkatpura (25 ntu.), M.G. Road (25 ntu.) and in south Toda (25 ntu.) the turbidity is beyond the permissible limit.

Fluoride

Excessive presence of fluoride in groundwater and its health effects have become a major geo-environmental issue in many parts of the world. In India the main source of fluoride in water are different fluoride bearing rocks. The maximum permissible limit of fluoride in drinking water is recommended to be 1.5mg/l by WHO. When present in high concentration it causes dental fluorasis (teeth), skeletal flurosis (bones) non-skeleton manifestations (soft tissues and organs) and even paralysis. It is important to note from Table 19.1 that Indore's groundwater quality in fluoride context is quite good. In India fluoride presence in groundwater is widespread, about 199 district are in danger from drinking water excess flouride (cf. UNICEF study)

Chloride

Chloride in the form of chloride ion (Cl^-) is one of the major inorganic anion in natural water and waste water. In potable water, the salty taste produced by chloride concentrations is variable and dependent on the chemical composition of water. The chloride concentration is higher in domestic sewage than in raw water because sodium-chloride (NaCl) is a common item of diet and passes unchanged through the digestive system. In drinking water the permissible limit is 250-1000 mg/l. From chloride point of view Indore's groundwater quality is not objectionable.

Nitrate

Nitrate is the highest oxidized from of nitrogen and in water its most important source is biological oxidation of nitrogenous organic matter of both autochthonous allochthonous origin. Domestic sewage contain very high amount of nitrogens compounds. High nitrate content (>40mg NO3 –N/1) may cause blue baby disease. Many groundwaters have significant quantities of nitrates coming from the percolating water. Sewage and other water is rich in nitrates. The permissible limit is 45mg/maximum nitrate in potable water. In Indore some of the residential areas are quite good as they do not have nitrate in their water but in high population concentration areas e.g. Juna Risala (100mg/max. as nitrate), Katkatpura (100mg/ max

Table 19.1: Quality of Groundwater in Indore City

S. No.	Selected Areas	Sample Collection Points	Temperature in °C	pH	Turbidity ntu	Fluoride mg/l	Chloride mg/l	Nitrate mg/l mg/l	Iron mg/l	Hardness	Ammonia mg/l	Faecal
A.	Residential	1. Juna Risala	26	7	<10	0.6	124.07	100	0.3	200	1.0	P
		2. Vaidya Khayliram Marg	25	7	10	0.6	425.40	<10	0.3	400	1.0	A
		3. Katkatpura	26	8	25	0.6	248.15	100	0.3	400	1.0	P
		4. Residency Well	25	7	10	0.6	124.07	Nil	0.3	400	1.0	P
		5. New Palasia	25	7	10	0.6	60.26	Nil	0.3	260	1.0	A
B.	Commercial	6. Jawahar Marg	26	7	10	0.6	354.65	Nil	0.3	400	1.0	A
		7. Cloth Market	27	7	10	0.6	109.85	<10	0.3	400	1.0	A
		8. Malharganj	26	7	10	0.6	120.53	100	0.3	280	2.0	A
		9. M.G. Road	31	8	25	0.6	283.60	<10	0.3	280	2.0	A
		10. Chhawani	26	7	10	0.6	127.62	<10	0.3	40	2.0	A
C.	Industrial	11. Sanwer Road A Sector	25	8	10	0.6	301.32	100	0.3	400	1.0	A
		12. Sanwer Road B Sector	26	8	10	0.6	453.76	100	0.3	400	1.00	P
		13. Sanwer Road F Sector	26	7	10	0.6	655.82	100	0.3	400	1.0	P
		14. Sanwer Road H Sector	25	8	10	0.6	195.00	100	0.3	400	2.0	A
		15. Sanwer Road T Sector	25	7	10	0.6	709.00	100	0.3	400	1.0	A
D.	Slums	16. South Toda	28	7	25	0.6	166.61	100	0.3	360	1.0	P
		17. Pancham Ki Phel	27	8	10	0.6	230.43	100	0.3	500	2.0	P
		18. Musakhedi	26	7	10	0.6	177.25	100	0.3	172	3.07	—
		19. Lala Ka Bagicha	23	7	10	0.6	319.05	100	0.3	400	2.0	P
		20. Lal Bag	26	7	10	0.6	230.42	100	0.3	360	1.0	—

Source: Field Observation and Testing, Year 2006,
P = Present, A = Absent

as nitrate) and in Industrial and slum area (each area is having 100mg/max as nitrate) it is on the danger line.

Iron

On the basis iron of iron content Indore city has a good water quality because in all areas of the city iron content is 0.3mg/l which is in permissible limit of the elements that makeup the earth crust, iron is the fourth most abundant by weight. Iron may be present in water in varying quantities, dependent upon the geology of the area and other chemical component of the watering.

Hardness

Hardness is the property of water which prevents lather formulation when using soap and increases the Boiling point of water. Hardness is principally due to the presence of calcium and magnesium cations. However, other cations such as stronium, iron and magnesium also contribute to hardness. Hardness is called temporary if it is caused by bicarbonate and carbonate salts of the cation and it can be removed simply by boiling the water. Permanent hardness is caused mainly by sulphates and chlorides of the metals. Hardness can be expressed in following manner:

Soft Water	0–75 Mg/l
Medium Water	75–150 Mg/l
Hard Water	150–300 Mg/l
Very Hard	> 300 Mg/l

In Indore the groundwater is of temporary hardness type. In industrial area the water is very hard because its value is 400 mg/l, Table 19.1. Similarly in slum areas some parts have very hard water e.g. Paneham ki Phel, and Lala ka Bagicha. In residential areas and commercial areas the water is hard or very hard.

Ammonia

Ammonia comes to groundwater mainly through human activities and natural decay process. Presence of Ammonia signifies organic pollution. It also indicates a recent origin of sewage pollution. Its permissible limit in drinking water is 1.5 mg./l but in Indore city some of the commercial areas are having 3.0 mg/l (Malharganj), 200 mg/l (M.G. Road and Chhawani). In the industrial areas it is 2.0 mg/l (H sector). Ammonia is quite common in the groundwater of slum areas e.g. it is 2.0 mg/l in Pancham ki Phel, > 3.0 mg/l in Moosakhedi and 2.0 mg/l in Lala ka Bagicha. It is harmful to human beings as well as fish and other biotic population.

If a drinking water supply, such as a stream or a shallow well, becomes polluted with human wastes (faeces, night soil, sewage, even some sewage effluents) it may serve as vehicle of transmission of such water borne diseases as typhoid, cholera and dysentary. In India several observing points have this serious problem e.g. Juna Risala, Katkatpura and Residency well. Some commercial areas e.g. Malharganj Industrial Areas and Slum areas are the affected areas of this problem (Table 19.1).

From the above discussion it is quite clear that the quality of water is not the same in all areas of Indore city. Some areas are having defective groundwater quality for e.g. Juna Risala, Katkatpura and Residency well of residential area. Juna Risala and Katkatpura of Juni Indore are densiely populated areas of the Holkar State. Lines are also very old and leakage problem occurs frequently.

In rainy season water logging is the main problem of these areas. In these circumstances groundwater quality is very poor. Residency well is in a posh area of Indore City. But the well is quite old (year 1856). It is necessary to clean and deepen the well.

In some commercial areas (Malharganj) the groundwater quality is not as good as it is required because this type of area is a densely populated compact and old area. Sewage lines are not proper. Pipe lines are broken in some places and this also creates problems.

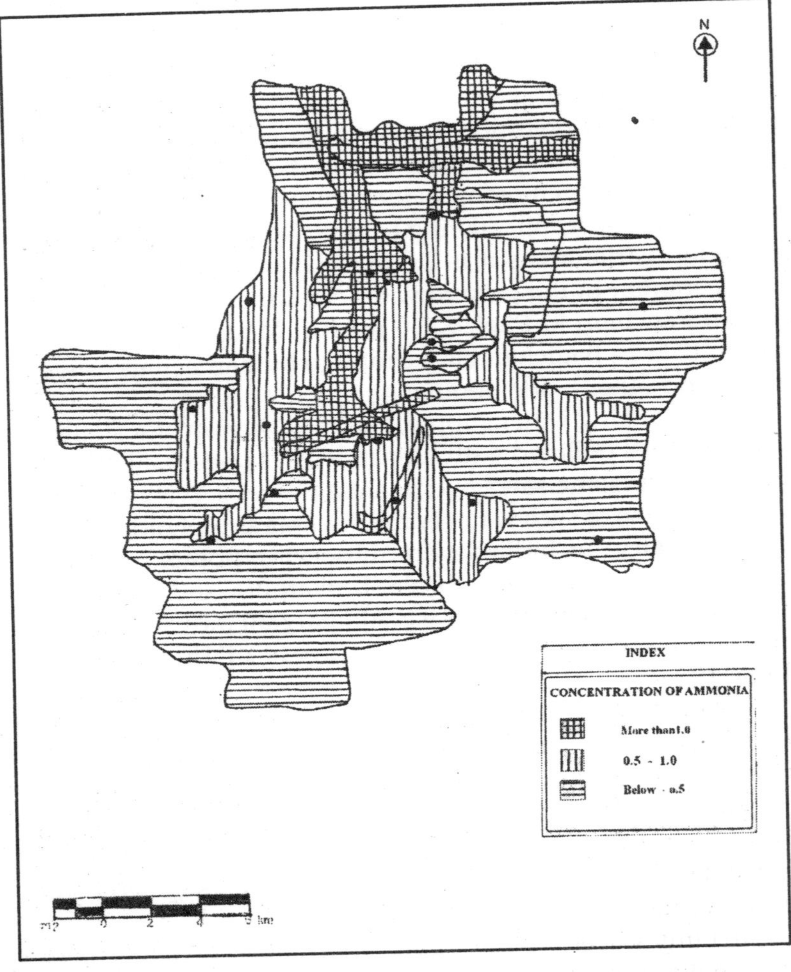

Fig. 19.3: Indore City : Concentration of Ammonia in Groundwater

Industrial and slum areas also have poor quality because of the chemical industrial units. While river Khan is almost a nallah of drainage water. Across the river most of the slums are flourshing, it results in pollution. The tubewells which are not so deep (100 feet) are getting polluted. The depth of tubewells and wells is also a criteria for pollution.

Conclusion

In India almost 85 per cent of drinking water needs are met from groundwater. The rapid exploitation of groundwater has caused depletion resulting in shortage of water supply and cause damage to its quality.

Identifying problems is of course much easier than suggesting solutions. However, following are some of the solutions to the problem which require detailed considerations.

(i) In old areas of the city the sewage lines are to be well maintained, leakage to be topped and regular monitoring is required or also new sewage lines to be laid whenever possible.

(ii) Guidelines for optimum exploitation of groundwater resources be strictly followed.

It is reported that a big loan from the World Bank is being negotiated and it may be hoped that such a beautiful city will be cured of pollution of at least drinking water.

REFERENCES

Indore Development Plan, 2021.

Chandrakumar, G. and N. Mukundan (Editors) *Water Resource Management : Trust and Challenges,* Sarupal Sons, New Delhi, 2006.

Saxena, M.M., *Handbook of Water and Soil Analysis,* Nidhi Publications Bikaner Year 2001.

Manivaskam, N. *Physico Chemical Examination of Sewage and Industrial Effluents.*

20

Quality of Air in Indore City

SUBHRA BISWAS AND D. KAUR

Introduction

The chapter examines the quality of air of Indore City during a time span of around six years and suggests planning measures to improve the quality of urban environment.

Objectives

The main objectives of this chapter are:

1. To review the state of ambient air, the changes in the quality of air over the last six years over Indore City.
2. To evaluate the peak hour traffic volume and corresponding air pollution at major locations of the city.
3. To suggest some planning measures to improve the quality of urban environment.

Database and Methodology

The available air quality data at major locations of Indore for a span of six years serve as the major data source in this study. Data sources include both primary and secondary sources. Secondary data has been collected from the office of Central Pollution Control Board and Road Transport Office, Indore.

Primary data been generated through personal observations at selected locations of the city.

The study is also supported by graphical representations of time series data.

Study Area

Indore is known as the commercial capital of Madhya Pradesh. With expanding business activities and consequent rise in income the motor vehicle population tends to increase at a high rate. This is true for both the two wheelers and four wheeler vehicles. In addition public transport demand adds a fleet of buses and three wheelers to the transport system of the study area.

It has been observed that the quality of air of Indore City is directly related to the transport sector followed by waste generation and industries. These are the main sources of particulate matter emissions. It may be added that commuters formulate their vehicular preferences based on differences in performance, convenience of travel, travel time, cost involved, safety and other factors. However, few travel choices are motivated by level of resource consumption, pollution control or local weather change concerns. The rising trend in motor vehicles ownership in the city particularly, that of two-wheelers, and diesel operated cars, supports this argument.

Figure 20.1 depicts the growth of vehicles in Indore along with the level of different pollutants in the air. In the study area private vehicles consist of cars, scooters/motorcycles/ mopeds, etc. Commercial vehicles combine a mix of heavy vehicles, taxis, three-wheelers, mini-trucks, buses and others like jeep, tractors, etc. According to standard norms, public transport in a city is expected to cover substantially higher vehicle kilometrage than private vehicles. But in Indore, the number of private vehicles is quite high compared to public vehicles (Fig. 20.1). It can be easily ascertained that the pollution load contributed per vehicle by the private transport is the major contributor of pollutants load. However, the number and density of public vehicles varies at different zones of Indore.

In the Central area, Agra-Mumbai road, public buses, *Nagar-Sewa* have quite frequent runs particularly during the peak traffic hours.

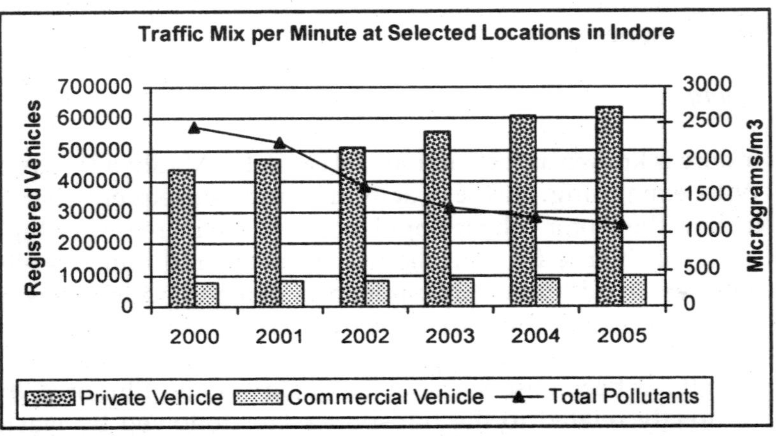

Fig. 20.1: Year-wise Growth of Vehicle Population in Indore and the changes in overall Ambient Air Quality

It may be mentioned that at different locations of the city, the volume of autos, tempos and other buses vary in different proportions. The number of two-wheelers has superseded (in terms of road space consumption) other modes in all the commercial areas. This is particularly true at Kothari Market and Palasia Square, Regal Square, etc. where cars, mini buses, autos, tempos have been largely outnumbered by two-wheelers. The per minute traffic mix estimated (through personal observations) provides a first hand evidence to this effect (Fig. 20.2).

The Pollutants of concern in Indore are mainly TSPM & RSPM

The Central Pollution Control Board has notified the 'National Ambient Air Quality Standards' (NAAQS) for various pollutants. Annual and 24-hourly average standards are fixed for SO_2, NO_x, SPM, RSPM (size less than 10 microns), lead (Pb), ammonia (NH3). One and 8-hourly standards are fixed for CO.

Different sets of standards are prescribed for industrial areas, residential, rural and other areas, sensitive areas etc. which are based on land use pattern.

In Indore, TSPM and RSPM are believed to be the main pollutants. Transport sector is believed to be a large contributor to urban PM levels due to special vehicle mix. For all sorts of pollutants, a mass reduction in emissions is estimated to be 54.36 per cent over the period of last 5/6 years. Smaller reduction is anticipated for RSPM and NO_x. It is due to the nature of traffic-mix and related emission levels (Fig. 20.2) at various locations. Two-wheelers are proportionately high in number at all locations followed by four wheelers and autos. At Pologround heavy vehicles outnumber other modes of traffic.

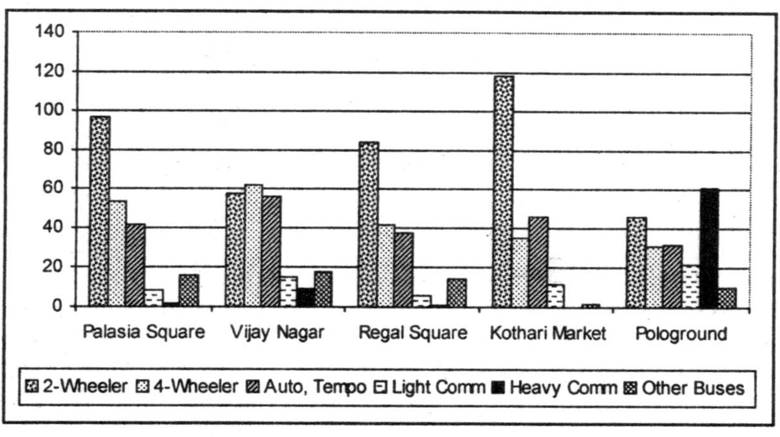

Fig 20.2: Traffic mix/minute at some selected locations in the Indore city

It may be mentioned that due to advancements in technology emission levels have shown a decreasing tendency as well. The (Fig. 20.3) shows an increasing trend in RSPM level between 2003 and 2004 for the residential areas. Between 2003 and 2004 the decrease was more pronounced in the Industrial area. There have been significant reductions in emission of SO_2 from all energy combustion sectors. Reductions in SO_2 are largely due to improvements in the combustion in energy and other industry sectors. Although the level of SO_2 got reduced in absolute figure in all sorts of land use zones; the percentage contribution from the transport sector (the emission level at major commercial and residential locations taken together) has remained almost constant over the last six years. It thus bears a testimony to the continuous rise in traffic volume on city roads.

The major reduction in emission of NO_x occurs in the combustion process in energy and road transport sectors. An increase in level of NO_x from 60.7 to 62.8 per cent in commercial and residential areas of Indore is also a clear indication of rising growth of traffic volume and a greater level of auto emissions. The RSPM level has also increased from a little over 57 per cent to 60.2 per cent. The main sources of RSPM or PM_{10} are linked with industrial, road transport and waste sectors. As new technologies continue to penetrate the market, emissions from road transport are projected to fall appreciably between 2000 and 2010.

The given graph represents the percentage changes in RSPM concentration in the overall pollution level in each of the three land use areas of the city.

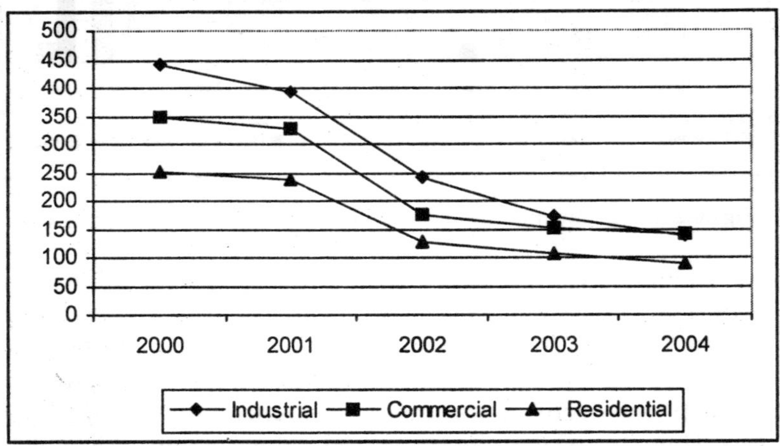

Fig. 20.3: Annual Average RSPM Concentrations in Different Land Use Areas in Indore

The pollutant level has also varied in the residential and commercial areas, with higher rise in commercial area of

Kothari Market (Figs. 20.4 and 20.5). Changes in land use in these areas are well reflected from these fluctuations in pollutants level.

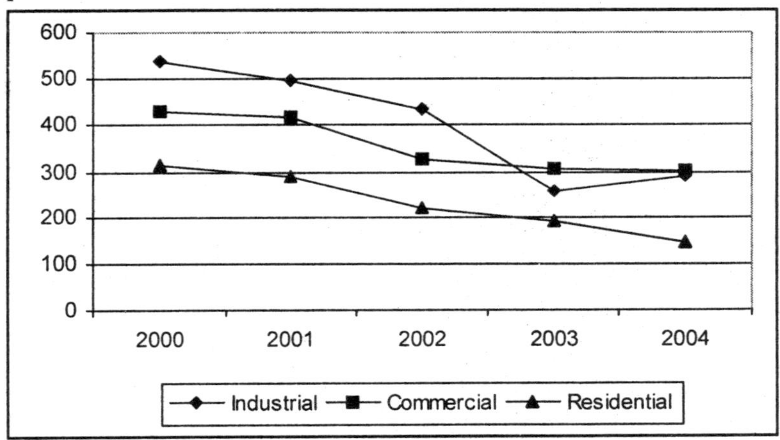

Fig 20.4: Annual Average TSPM Concentration in Major Land Use Areas in Indore

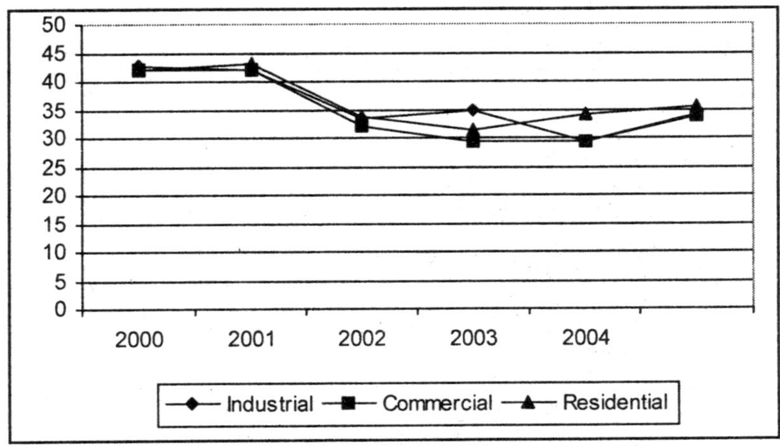

Fig 20.5: RSPM as a Percentage of Total Pollutants in Indore City

Air Quality Standards and Exceedence Factor

Historically, the National ambient air quality standard has differed by land use, with the most stringent standards set for "sensitive" areas, followed by "residential, rural and other areas" and the most lenient standard for "industrial" areas. The graphs given below Figs. 5(a) and (b) show the temporal change, based on annual average values, when the level of TSPM and RSPM are above the standard norms in each of the three land use areas.

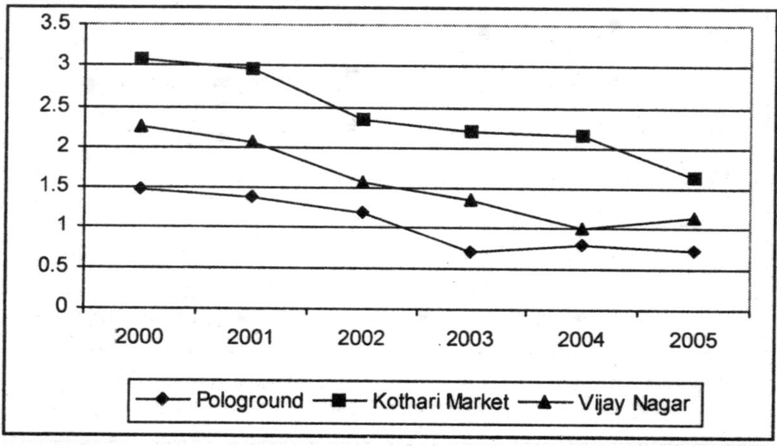

Fig 20.5(a): Exceedence Factor of TSPM in Ambient Air at Major Locations

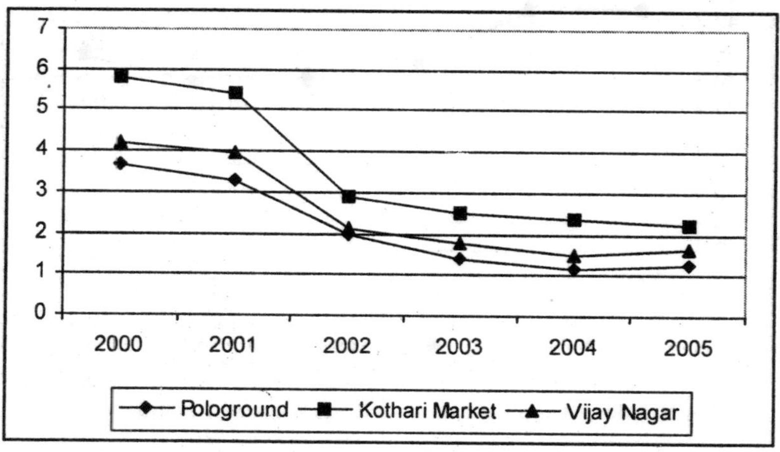

Fig. 20.5(b): Exceedence Factor of PM_{10} in Ambient Air at Major Locations

In order to give a better insight into this finding, the monthly average values criteria of pollutants for the year 2005 has been considered. The exceedence factor calculated on its basis, ranged from low to very high groups as shown in the Table 20.1. The monthly incidence of exceedence factor gives a somewhat close justification of exceedence level of pollutants in commercial and residential locations, over the last six years. The Table 20.1 represents the pollution index of TSPM and RSPM categorized as very high, high, moderate and low in the respective land use areas.

Table 20.1 : Pollution Index of TSPM and RSPM

Location	*Pollutant*	*Low 0-1.0*	*Medium 1.0–2.0*	*High 2.0-3.0*	*Severe/ Very High 3.0 and above*
Pologround	TSPM	10	2	—	—
	PM_{10}	3	9	—	—
Kothari Market	TSPM	3	5	4	—
	PM_{10}	—	4	5	3
Vijay Nagar	TSPM	3	9	—	—
	PM_{10}	2	8	2	—

It is quite surprising that a major commercial zone of Indore has experienced a steady decrease in level of all sorts of pollutants in its ambient air. Of the three major land use areas, where air quality is measured, the maximum improvement in the level of RSPM is observed in Industrial area, 42.88 per cent to 29.38 per cent, between 2000 and 2005.The minimum improvement is recorded in Vijay Nagar, Telephone Nagar residential area—42.07 to 34.08 per cent during the same time. The TSPM concentration in Industrial area fell from 563 $\mu g/m^3$ in 2000 to 258 in 2003 and then increased to 289 in 2004 with a little reduction in 2005.

Compared to 2004, the RSPM level increased in 2005—by 9.88 per cent (139 to 152.7 $\mu g/m^3$). The TSPM level also records an increase compared to 2003. The ongoing large-scale construction activities in these areas (which have witnessed a sprawled growth in recent times) can be hold responsible for the rise in particulate pollutants in the air. The residential area of Vijay Nagar have witnessed much growth over the last five-six years, with much construction activities and an overall rise in vehicular movements—private and commercial.

Conclusions

In Indore tighter emission standards and better fuel quality are responsible for much reduction of pollutants. However, the constant rise of traffic volume keeps the emission rate at a high level. This is particularly observed in the 2005 data, which shows slight increase in TSPM & RSPM levels in industrial and residential areas. The study is supported by level of exceedence of these pollutants above the defined standard. In all the cases, there is a marked increase in the proportion of RSPM in 2005 compared to 2004. The chapter seeks to find the possible causes for changes in pollution level in each of the land use areas under study and puts forward some proposals for pollution mitigation.

A Brief Plan for Pollution Mitigation

In general the air quality monitoring programme needs to be improved. In Indore, transport sector is the most threatening source of air pollution. In order to overcome the transport related problems, some associated aspects need special attention of planners. Public Transport as the most viable mode, needs to be facilitated by road segregation. Separate lanes for fast moving vehicles and two-wheelers including cycling paths; road widening in the central parts of the city; construction of flyovers; installation of red lights control according to traffic volume at several intersections could be of immense help in easing out traffic and lowering emissions levels at selected points. Moreover, peoples' participation and road awareness level need to be improved in these directions.

REFERENCES

1. The World Bank, Environment and Social Development Unit, South Asia Region, for a Breath of Fresh Air—1993-2002.
2. R.K. Bose, Urban Transport and Environment Problems and Policies, India Infrastructure Summit, March, 2005, New Delhi.
3. D. Mohan, G. Tiwari, "Sustainable Transport Systems: Linkages Between Environmental Issues, Public Transport, Non-motorized Transport and Safety", *Economic and Political Weekly*, Vol XXXIV: 25, 1999, pp. 1589-1596.

21

Depletion of Groundwater in Indore City

SHOBHA SHARMA

Environmental hazards may be categorized in to two types. Firstly there are environmental hazards which are noticed visibly and which leave an imprint on the earth through the destruction of life and property. These hazards may be in the form of volcanic eruption, earthquake, landslide, storm. cyclone, tsunami waves, floods, drought and so on. On the other hand there are environmental hazards that keep on creeping with surreptitiousness. These may not be visibly noticed in routine life but in course of time become more devastating than the hazards, which are easily noticed and felt. The depletion of groundwater is one such natural hazard that has been discussed in this chapter in context of Indore city.

Water, the elixir of life, is being exploited enormously now a days. We are very close to the popular saying "Water, water everywhere but not a drop to drink". Water comprises nearly 71 per cent of the total earth area but even than the world is facing scarcity of water and the future situation seems to be very grim. It is known that the major sources of fresh water are surface water bodies e.g. lakes, pools, puddles, ponds, rivers, streams, springs, etc. Apart from these people also rely upon groundwater sources as wells and tubewells. Maximum amount of water on the earth is out of reach of the mankind as it is not in directly usable form, i.e. ocean water, ice caps and atmospheric water vapor. Hence majority of our water requirements are fulfilled through precipitation.

Water Management in Indore City

Water management is a global issue. Madhya Pradesh in general and Malwa region in particular is also facing an alarming water crisis situation since last one decade due to infrequent and insufficient monsoon rains. Government agencies and local bodies are trying to explore alternative sources of water which are costly, economically and environmentally.

Indore is the biggest city of Madhya Pradesh denoted as commercial capital of the State. The population of this city is increasing logarithmically. Initially Indore was dependent on Yashwant Sagar, Bilawali, Piplyapala, Sirpur, so many water bodies. Later on water is fetched uphill from a distance of 65 km from river Narmada which seems insufficient now. Narmada water has been brought to Indore in two phases and efforts for the third phase are still on. Modernization of living and construction of huge residential colonies have necessitated construction of private wells and tubewells to meet the growing demand of drinking water (Table 21.1). This over exploitation of water is a result of increasing population, modernization of life style, infrastructure development, dispersion, development across the borderline, continuously surrounding *panchayats* and villages being included in the city area. These factors have created growing demand for fresh water on sources of availability of fresh water in Indore city.

Table 21.I: Tube-wells and Hand Pumps in Indore City

Zone	*Tubewells*	*Hand Pumps*	*Wells*
1-3	866	117	3
4-6	707	112	31
7-9	562	117	27
10-12	562	769	34

N.B. : 2904 Tubewells, 481 hand pumps, 95 wells to be repaired.

Consequences of Over Drawing Groundwater

The pressing demand on underground water resources of the city is sending distress signals so far as the availability of drinking water in the city is concerned. Some of the consequences may be outlined as under.

Falling Water Tables and Depletion

The availability of groundwater for a long-term sustenance depends on the balance between input rates and output rates. When withdrawal rates exceed recharge rates the water table drops and eventually the groundwater of the area is depleted. The lateral flow of groundwater is generally very slow because water percolates through porous material and may be precluded altogether by various rock formations. Therefore, the groundwater may be depleted in one area but still present in a nearby area. In Indore there was very good monsoon season and sufficient rainfall occurred during the past decade. It lead to an increase in ground water level. At the same time gradually annual precipitation decreases due to deforestation, growing urbanization leading to ferro concrete structures and new roads being laid down regularly. The expansion of the city area is encroaching agricultural and forest land. Regular alteration in natural topography has prevented the percolation of water and maximum amount of rain water is drained as runoff for the lack of proper sites for groundwater recharge. These are some of the important factors which are responsible for the decline of ground water level in Indore.

There is a differential ratio for drawing groundwater and recharging rate is also imbalanced so it has created the problem of availability of groundwater in Indore. Tubewells are gradually drying up and some of them have totally dried up. The increased use of groundwater for irrigation in the surrounding areas of Indore also caused the depletion of water table. The recent growth and prosperity of the city is based on overdrawing groundwater and it will cause falling water table at the rate approaching 2m/year. This rate may result in almost total depletion of drinking water within the next 20 years.

Diminishing Surface Water

Surface water bodies play a major role for the maintenance of ground water when the source of water for inland water bodies are diverted or insufficiently fed it brings less water to these bodies. The water bodies like Yashwant Sagar, Bilawali, Piplyapala, Sirpur in Indore are also facing this problem. Apart from whatever amount of water is received by these water bodies, water does not remain for long as people draw this water through pumping sets for various purposes and water bodies start drying some times even in late winter months which has great bearing on groundwater as well as on aquatic flora and fauna thriving there.

Excessive groundwater use and digging at depth provides hard and mineral water which may contain fluorides and arsenic which are toxic for life.

Land Subsidence

Over the ages groundwater has leached cavities in the earth. These spaces filled with water play a crucial role in supporting the overlying rocks and soil. This leads to a gradual setting of land, a phenomenon known as land subsidence. The sinkage rate may be 3 to 30 cm per year. Land subsidence causes building foundation, road ways, water and sewer lines to crack. Another kind of subsidence is the occurrence of a sink hole which may be sudden. A sink hole results when an underground cavern in drained of its supporting ground water suddenly collapse. Sink holes may 100m or more across as much as 50m deep.

Conclusion

In order to maintain groundwater level there should be one boring in one region which is connected to 25-30 homes run for short time. Borings should be registered with details of depth and location. Boring which are useless should be sealed. Older wells and ponds should be treated for pure water and their depth should be increased. Rainwater harvesting should be made obligatory in all residential areas particularly in new colonies. Efforts need to be made for water recharging through plantation programmes and water conservation measures. Means like public awareness programmes and related education should be adopted.

SECTION-E

PUBLIC IMAGE

22

Environment, Social Concern and Initiative—A Bird's Eye View (A Brief of Hindi Equivalent)

SAROJ YADAV

Introduction

Land, water, fire, air and sky (void, vacant space) are the five macroscopic elements (*Panch Mahabhoot*) which constitute the entire infrastructure of all the living and the non-living in the universe. The constituent material should be free from any foreign grain, pollution and adulteration so that the creation is sustained and regulated in a graceful functional dignity,in every form and figure. All the living (biotic) and non-living (abiotic) objects held in a surrounding invariably influence one another. All the living and non-living objects in our surrounding and their interaction is collctively called environment.

Component of Environment

There are two components of environment—living (biotic) and non-living (abiotic). The living components include, among others, human beings, animals, birds, plants, bacteria, organism and fungi. The non-living components include, among others, air, water, land, fire, sky, light, heat, temperature and rainfall. All the living things essentially need food for their growth, development and survival. All the living beings are linked to one another by a food-chain. Green plants are the only organism that manufacture their food themselves, from the material available in nature. Plants consume carbon-dioxide gas and release oxygen gas. Animals and human beings consume oxygen and release carbon dioxide. The cycle maintains gaseous equilibrium in nature. Nutrients and minerals sustain living organism by adequate supply of energy. The cycling of nutrients or minerals occurs from the living to non-living components and vice-versa. The environment, under these interactions, is maintained dynamic in nature. A balance is automatically struck in nature if the activity is not hampered and impeded by extrinsic influences.

Vedic Directives and Guiding Principles

Since the dawn of civilization, the four *Vedas* have issued multiple directives to human beings for upholding sanctity and holyness of components of environment. Pious and pure should these benevolent factors be maintained for achieving the general welfare of mankind and living beings. The *Agnihotra* is a traditional anti-pollution ritual to be performed daily by a householder. Its objective is to keep the environment neat and clean, healthy and congenial. The *Panch-Mahabhoot* are treated as adorable deities. Respect and reverence of highest order are paid to them in all walks of life, in all shades and circumstances.

Resources

The components and the aspects of environment which provide the means for growth, development and survival of human life are called resources. Infact, the human being himself is a resource. He produces as well consumes the various available features and factors of environment. Water, air and land are the three basic resources provided by nature. Air is the most precious natural resource on earth. Life-cycle began in water. Water is an extremely essential commodity required for survival of all biotic life. Land is a valuable resource upon which humanity depends for its supply of food, fibre and fuel. The resources can be classified as renewable and non-renewable.

The renewable sources can be continuously replenished and reproduced in nature in a cyclic flow. Air, water, soil, sunlight, agricultural produce, forest and living being, among many others, belong to renewable category. Coal, petroleum, oil, natural gas, metals, diamonds represent some resources that belong to non-renewable category. They cannot be produced in nature at a perpetual pace in a rapid sequence. Their production involves a time-consuming, tedious and elaborate exercise.

Ecosystem

Ecology deals with the study of interactions between living beings and the environment. Ecosystem operates as an active cycle wherein lies an exchange of energies. Energy is defined as capacity of doing work. Urbanization, industrialization, population-explosion and widespread poverty have produced an imbalance in the ecosystem. The notorious effect is enhanced due to hunger and poverty among the bereaved and the down-trodden. The prosperous regions, on the other hand, are reaping fruits beyond proportion. The eco-system ruptures with a formidable note and warns of alarming consequences. The balance can be restored by a universal wish and will.

Pollution

Pollution means a deterioration in quality of one or many components of environment leading to adverse influence on living beings. Extensive use of fertilizers and pesticides, to get bumper crops, causes land pollution. The industrial and chemical wastes pollute water in rivers, lakes, seas and oceans. The oil-spills from the ships cover the sea surface and drag marine life towards termination. The burning of coal and the vehicular emissions are the main causes of air pollution. The smoke contains carbon-monoxide, sulphur-dioxide and nitrogen oxide gases. Mixture of such obnoxious gases, with water in the atmosphere, may culminate into acid rains. Ozone umbrella, against ultraviolet rays, provides protection to terrestrial activity and checks global warming. Air-conditioners and refrigerators eject harmful gases like chloro-fluoro-carbon (CFC) which pierce the ozone cover. The consequences paint a horrible and terrible picture for future. The advancement in technology and the towering requirements of energy are responsible for generation of many kinds of wastes. Their successful disposal poses a huge problem to human kind. Waste can be defined as a material which has been rejected for further use in a system. It causes environmental problems. The waste can neither escape into atmosphere nor can be eliminated through flowing waters. Radioactive waste presents a long-term threat to public health. Stress is laid on three R's-reduce, reuse and recycle before the waste is disposed off. Beware, the waste may not mar the rest.

Environment Protection Act

For environment protection, the Government of India have framed and formulated the following acts:

(i) The Wildlife (Protection) Act, 1972.
(ii) The Water (Prevention and Control of Pollution) Act, 1974.
(iii) The Forest (Conservation) Act, 1980.
(iv) The Environment (Protection) Act, 1986.

This highligh to the care, concern and consideration of the government.

Conclusion

The world observers Environment Day on 5th June every year. India, on world-forum, pronounced and postulated its firm belief that the most important factor responsible for environment deteoration is pollution due to poverty. Perhaps the public awareness, dissemination and diffusion of relevant education and elimination of poverty may yield the desired result at the world-forum.

SECTION-F

ABSTRACTS OF HINDI PAPERS PRESENTED IN THE SEMINAR AND RECOMMENDATIONS

I

Bio-diversity and Conservation of Environment

*ANURADHA MISHRA

Present study deals with the importance of Bio-diversity to the society. It also focuses attention towards Bio-diversity in India. India is a multi-biodiversity country, having 45,000 types of species of plants. India has versatile physical features. This also supports different type of plants and animals. Increasing population is a world-wide problem. It is affecting bio-diversity rapidly. Paper also suggests some conservation action to prevent bio-diversity specially forest conservation.

* Asst. Prof. of Home Science,Government P.G. Girls' College Motitabela Indore

II

Temporal Studies of Climatic Changes in Indore City

*MANISHA LAVANSHI, PRIYANKA YOGI, PARAG MESHRAM, ANKUSH KHOBRAGADE and NAVITA RAJURKAR

The study presents a detailed scenario of climate with reference to Indore city. It is a Temporal study since the analysis is based upon the climatic data viz. temperature and rainfall of last 31 years. For this purpose secondary data is collected at the local level. It is observed that temperature and rainfall of this region are fluctuating in other words trend of these features are irregular, unreliable and unexpected due to Global warming. Temperature is observed to be on increase in those months when previously it was quite low and at the same time decrease in those months when it was very high.

* All research scholars M.Phil Deptt., School of Advanced Liberal Studies, D.A.V.V. Indore.

III

Perception and Usefulness of Forest Resources—A Case Study of Village Nahar, Jhabua and Tillore Khurd

*Rakhi Shukla

Forests are an important component of our environment and economy , besides this forests check air pollution and soil erosion and maintain ecological balance. Unfortunately the forest wealth is vanishing at a rapid rate and deforestation is becoming a big environmental problem. With these views, present study deals with 'forest perception' means human being's view towards the forests.

The study aims at forest usefulness among rural people who depend or reside close to forests. It also studies view of those people who are related with forest resources and analyses the factors responsible for forest development. The study is based upon the primary source of information of Indore tehsil, Madhya Pradesh.It analyses forest usefulness with reference to wood, grass, Tendupatta, food material, medicines and building material and finds out the impact of forest products in terms of income pattern. The study highlights the views of surveyed families regarding the effect of forest on environment. It concludes that types and availability of forest products affects forest usefulness and at the same time knowledge of forest usefulness sometime harmful for forest eco-system.

* Asst. Prof. of Geography , Government P.G. Girls'College, Motitabela, Indore M.P.

IV

Problem of Slums: Social Degradation with Special Reference to Ujjain City of M.P.

* Saishwari Kaul

Present study deals with many burning issues of slums. Their cancerous growth is a great problem for modern civilized cities. Rapid urbanization is responsible for this phenomenon. Ujjain city is an ancient holy city of Madhya Pradesh. The study is based on primary and secondary sources of data. 4 slums are selected at random for the analysis. It aims to know the growth of population and economic status of the slums.

Some suggestions regarding improvement in social environment viz. increase in employment opportunities, establishment of government societies, awareness with relation to family planning, cleaning concept between slum dwellers and punishment for crimes are suggested.

* Asst. Prof. & Head. Nehru Government P.G. College, Agar Malwa Distt. Sajapur, Madhya Pradesh

V

Organic Farming for Environmental Security with Reference to Kasturbagram

*MANOJ SANWALE, JITENDRA THAKUR, MISS RANI VASKEL, SANDHYA SOLANKI and ANITA PANDARE

Organic farming is the demand of the present chemical farming creating various types of environmental imbalances. Organic farming can delimit it, which is incidentally a part of our traditional farming system.

Present study is based upon primary and secondary sources of information. Kasturbagram institute is a research centre of agriculture. Organic farming has the capacity to break the life cycle of microorganisms, insects and pests, not only that it also conserves soil, water, forest and bio-diversity.

* All M.Phil Research Scholars, School of Advanced Liberal Studies, Devi Ahilya, Vishwavidyalaya, Indore (M.P.)

VI

Slums and Environmental Degradation in Indore Metropolis

*DEVENDRA KAUR and **SHUCHI VERMA

Urbanization and Industrialization are the sources of prosperity and development but at the same time these factors responsible for the degradation of social environment in terms of development of slums. Present study aims at the study of the infrastructural facilities of slums and its effect on environment. For this purpose types of family, house types, cast analysis, road, health and recreation facilities, employment and income structure have been observed in randomly selected families of slums.

Present study reveals that Indore city was an example of beauty, security and cleanliness but nowadays it is suffering from cancerous growth of slums. Concentration of industries, commerce and trading activities are responsible for this problem. It is observed that slum dwellers are lacking drinking water facilities, hospitals, proper sewage system, and road facilities. Solid waste material is another problem of this area. The solution is in slum dwellers hand. They can only solve these problems.

* Prof. and Head, Department of Geography, Government Arts and Commerce College, Indore (M.P.)

** Ph.D. Research Scholar, Government Arts and Commerce College, Indore (M.P.)

VII

Role of Watershed Mission in the Natural Resource Management : A Case Study

*JULIET ONKAR and **REKHA VERMA

Watershed mission is a multipurpose programme for conservation of water. Main objectives of this mission are to control dried situations and available permanent opportunities for employment in rural areas with their background. Present study aims to analyze changes in agricultural land use, forestry and cropping pattern with proper implementation of this scheme.

The data sources are of secondary level. A case study of Nalchha Mili watershed of Dhar district, Madhya Pradesh has been taken for this purpose.

The study reveals some positive effects from launching this scheme such as the cultivated land has increased, uncultivated land decreased and fallow land also decreased which is a positive sign of development. The cropping pattern shows a marked increase in Kharif as well as Rabi cropping area. In short this mission made a positive change in the field of agricultural forestry, horticulture and soil conservation.

* Prof. of Geography, Government P.G. College, Mhow, M.P.
** Prof. of Geography, Government P.G. College, Mhow, M.P.

VIII

Organic Farming Innovation in Indore Tehsil : A Concrete Effort for Soil Conservation

*Pragati Bhokardhanker and **Nitin Chourasia

Present study aims to find out impacts due to utilization of organic fertilizers in selected villages of Indore Tehsil. Organic farming can restrict the soil degradation and chemical pollution in crops. The study is based upon primary as well as secondary sources of data. Selection of villages for the study is based upon random method. Bio-fertilizers and their working is dealt in detail in the present study.

The study concludes that organic manure is a cheap and clean source of environment, as it is made by vegetation , cow dung, cow urine, honey butter etc. In high innovative villages organic and green manure are found. Least innovative villages are situated far away from urban centres and have least irrigation facilities. In high innovative villages modern irrigation system e.g. drip and shower are available in well developed condition. In these villages production is also constant, inspite of lack of rainfall in comparison to the other villages . It is found where there is organic farming practices are used, the fertility of the soil increased, insecticide application is not necessary, irrigation has become optional and the quality of food crop is growing better. This is a successful effort towards soil conservation.

* Asst. Prof. of Geography, Government Arts and Commerce College, Indore M.P.

** Guest Faculty, Geography Government Degree College, Bheekangaon, Dist. Khargone, M.P.

IX

Psychosomatic Effect of Thoughtful Environment

*PRAMODINI MONE

Present study focuses on a very typical environmental issue, i.e. Psychosomatic effect on mind and body , which is an abstract environment. Only matter does not affect Man's activity but circumstances and incidents also have their effect on person. Circumstances and their result form an environmental network. The study focuses on Man's Mental Development, thoughts attitude, behaviour, personality etc.

Man is a social animal right from the forest life to the modern highly developed city life, he has been a member of multi-faced mixed group. Customs affect him from birth and the society becomes his environment. Not only individuals but events also become the cause sometimes reliever and some times killer. He binds himself to the society. Developed society manifests itself in a developed individual, causing thought struggle leading to despondency, fear, anger etc. in a person, finally leading to chemical reaction influencing sympathetic autonomous nervous system, which we generally describe as mental distraction or tension.

* Asst. Prof., Government P.G. Girs' College, Motitabela, Indore, M.P.

X

Environment *versus* Art of Living

*Mayarani Devda

Present study deals with various sources of environmental problems viz. nuclear plants, radio activity, burning of fossils fuel, carbondioxide production from industrial units, decomposition of waste, carbon mono oxides, chlorofluoro-carbons from refrigeration, green house gases, ozone depletion etc.

Although India has been becoming one among the six major countries of atomic power and it has a very important place in this field but the environmental problems in the country are not very serious and alarming as our country has very few large scale industrial units, refrigeration systems and oil refineries or automatic vehicle system as compared to the other countries. In spite of all the trouble is that our people are lazy, lacking in proper knowledge and unsystematic.

The paper also deals with the drinking water problem in our country as well as land pollution.

* Asst. Prof., Geography, Government Arts and Science College, Ratlam, M.P.

XI

Environmental Pollution due to Religious Functions with Reference to Ujjain City

*SANDIP SARAWAN AND LOKESH SHARMA

Ujjain city is a famous religious city of not only Madhya Pradesh, but also of India and abroad. Everybody knows it's importance due to the famous "Mahakal Temple". Religious functions are very common in the city as it is a City of Temples.

Present study focuses due attention to the pollution problem which takes place because of religious programmes. It analyses major types of pollution viz. land pollution, water pollution , air pollution and soil pollution. Kshipra the great holy river is slowly and gradually slackening into a nullah of waste material mostly of the temples. Many Indian customs and rituals are performed across this river. The city is lacking in several essential facilities viz. trenching ground, management of solid waste, clean water etc. at present study suggests some remedial actions to solve these alarming problems

* M.Phil. Research Scholars, School of Advanced Liberal Studies,D.A.V.V. Indore (M.P.)

XII

Electronic Waste : A Serious Challenge for Environment.

*SUMITRA JOSHI AND KAVITA CHANDANI

This paper studies very serious issue of modern times viz. Electronic Waste. Electronic items are common in factories, offices, shops, industries, houses etc. In our country 75 per cent houses are having television sets, computers, CD/DVD Players, Video Cameras etc. They are now common items which are found in houses and institutions. These digital products create great problems.

E-Waste is not a world-wide problem but it is also an alarming one in space. India itself generates 1 lakh 46 thousand tones E-Waste every year. The latest reports of Environmental organizations show that India and China are dumping yards for the world's E-Waste. E-Waste contains many toxic matters, such as lead, mercury, cadmium, antimony, PVC plastic bromine etc. which create serious problems. It is the demand of time that we focus our serious attention towards these problems else the life on the earth will be impossible.

* Asst. Prof., MKHS Gujrati Girls' College Indore.

XIII

Environmental Pollution and Its Impact on the Tribal Populated Area.

*AJAY KUMAR RAI

Present study deals with the environmental pollution associated with the tribes of the country, especially tribal areas of Chhotanagpur plateau. In this region forests area is being reduced day-by-day and the tribal people fully dependent on their forests are suffering from this problem. Their existence is in danger. These tribes are our heritage of culture.

Paper also presents a critical picture of Korba industrial region. This region has an acute problem of air pollution due to the burning of coal. It is urgently necessary to solve these problems with the active participation of environmentalists, geographers, zoologists and activists in this field.

* Ph.D. Research Scholar, Baba Saheb Ambedkar, National Research Institute, Mhow, M.P.

XIV

Disposal of Urban Waste Water A Case Study of Indore City

*ARCHANA PUROHIT

Present study reveals with Urban Waste Water disposal—a burning issue of unplanned and haphazard urbanization in India. This has led to acute housing problem, increase in pollution, widespread dirt, poverty, lowering of standards of living and exploitation of land. Urbanization has increased the growth of population and the impact of industrialization is in the form of increase in the number of factories. But even today urban centres are lacking in the field of waste water management. There is no definite and systematic plan for waste water disposal.

Present study aims to study the disposal of urban waste water. It also analyses present sewage system of the city and problems associated with unplanned disposal of waste water. The study reveals that the quality of sewage water is decidedly very bad in condition but it is drained in some areas of the city without treatment and across these areas farmers are growing vegetables which are then sold in the city. It is also observed while testing that lead, arsenic, copper etc. are found in alarming quantity particularly in the vegetables . This is creating a big health hazard . It is therefore the demand of the time to take remedial actions without delay viz. launching underground sewage system and make treatment of wastewater.

* Asst. Prof. of Geography, Government Post Graduate College, Motitabela, Indore(M.P.)

XV

Indira Sagar Project : Problems of Rehabilitation—A Challenge to the Environment : A Case Study of Harsud

*Garima Dongre

Dams are the evidence of human development, but some times they create a big problem. Indira Sagar Project is also an evidence of Rehabilitation problems in the region.Present study focuses upon this issue with solid facts. Harsud town was in Khandwa district of Harsud tehsil, which is a victim of Indira Sagar Project.The study analyses environmental degradation due to the rehabilitation and degradation stresses upon actual rehabilitation.It also presents a comparative analysis with reference to some indices of old (Harsud) and new Harsud (Chhanera).

Present study is based upon the primary as well as secondary sources of data. Several parameters viz. population, length of roads, industries, land use etc. are taken for the analysis. The study reveals that in rehabilitated Harsud houses are not sufficient for Harsud's population.All green belts of old Harsud including dense forest are sub-merged.New railway line has destroyed fertile agricultural land.

Rehabilitation is not bad but at the cost of environmental degradation it costs dearly.

* Ph.D. Research Scholar, Government P.G. Girls' College, Indore.

Recommendations

VENU TRIVEDI

Government Post Graduate Girls' College, Motitabela, Indore, a leading educational institute of Indore hosted the National Conference entitled, "Environmental Problems and Intiatives" sponsored by University Grants Commission, Central Regional Office, Bhopal from 23rd to 24h February, 2007. The conference proceedings were organized in technical sessions, special lectures, and poster sessions. Altogether 100 research papers were presented by delegates. The conference also organized a competition for Best Research Paper Poster Session for young geographers (below 35 years). The poster session was organized in the sweet memory of late Prof. Vijaya Phanse, former Head, Department of Geography, Government Arts and Commerce College Indore. Dr. Manjula Choubey, the Patron of the conference and Principal of the college provided all facilities and encouragement to Dr. Venu Trivedi, the convener of the conference.

Delegates: A Profile

About 200 delegates from local and all parts of the country participated in the Technical Sessions. The delegates were drawn from Universities, Colleges, Institutes, Research and Development Organizations and Voluntary Organizations, etc. Distinguished geographers and environmentalists like Prof H.S. Sharma, President National Association of Geographers (NAGI), Jaipur (Raj.), Prof V.K. Shrivastava, Emeritus fellow, D.D.U. Vishwavidyalaya, Gorakhpur (U.P.), Prof. B.C. Vaidya, Head, Department of Geography, Pune University and

Secretary, The Deccan Geographical Society (D.G.S.) Pune (Maharashtra), Dr. S.M. Rashid, Deptt of Geography, Jamia Milia Islamia, New Delhi, Dr. T.A. Sihorawala, Retd. Prof. and Head Shri Govindram Sakseria Institute of Technological Science, Prof. Y.G. Joshi, Dean Baba Saheb Ambedkar National Institute, Mhow and Dr. K.R.Shrivastava Director, Geo marketing Laboratory, Gorakhpur (U.P).

Inaugural Session

The Inaugural Session of the National Conference on "Environmental Problems and Initiatives" was held on 23rd Feb 2007 at 10.00 a.m. in the college hall. Dr. M.K. Dad, Additional Director (Indore-Ujjain division), Higher Education, Government of M.P. was kind enough to preside as the Chief Guest. The dignitaries on the dais were Dr. B.C. Vaidya, Dr. H.S. Sharma, Dr. Manjula Choubey Principal and Patron of the event, Dr. Venu Trivedi, Head, Department of Geography of the College and convener of the conference. The session began with the worship of Goddess Saraswati.

The welcome address was delivered by Dr. Manjula Choubey followed by a brief introduction of guests by Dr. Venu Trivedi. She also highlighted the theme of the conference. The session was marked by the key note address on "Problems of desertification with special reference to Indian Desert" by Dr. H.S. Sharma. In this session a souvenir on "Environmental problems and initiatives" was released by Dr. N.K. Dad, Additional Director and the Chief Guest.

Mrs. Archana Purohit conducted the session and Dr. Sudha Kapoor presented the vote of thanks. The dignitaries and delegates later participated in a social meet.

Poster Session in memory of late Prof. Dr. Vijaya Phanse

After lunch a special feature of poster presentation competition was held in the Geography Department. The panel of judges for the competition was Prof V.K. Shrivastava Emeritus fellow, Gorakhpur (U.P.), Prof H.S. Sharma, Jaipur (Raj.) and Dr. B.C. Vaidya Pune (Maharashtra).

Miss Garima Dongre, Research Scholar, Department of Geography, Govt P.G. Girls College Motitabela, Indore was declared to be the winner. She presented her research paper by two posters on the "Indira Sagar Project; problems of rehabilitation—A challenge for environment, a case study of HARSUD". The competition was restricted for below 35 years of age of Scholars and lecturers. The competition was organized in loving memory of late Prof. Dr. Vijaya Phanse. Former Prof. and Head, of Department of Geography Government Arts and Commerce College, Indore. She was an innovative young lady, dedicated and sincere teacher of Geography. It is hoped young geographers will take lesson from her attitude and dedication to Geography.

TECHNICAL SESSION—I

Environmental Problems—Anthropogenic and Natural

The first technical session was devoted to "Environmental problems—Anthropogenic and Natural". The session was chaired by Prof. H.S. Sharma, Co-chaired by Dr.M.K. Oza, President, Indian Cartographic Association, Indore chapter; Dr. Devandra Kaur acted as rapporteur.

Prof. V. K. Shrivastava, Emeritus Fellow, Gorakhpur was the lead speaker in the session. He gave special lecture on, "Bio's Theory". Research papers followed this special lecture. In this session nearly 20 research papers were presented. The main issues of the discussion were Air pollution, Atomic energy, Causes of environmental problems, Thermal pollution, Chemical pesticides, Ground-water problems, Environment and Health and Music, Slums and environmental degradation, Health Hazards, Acid rain, Ethical environment etc. The papers were thoroughly discussed in this session.

Mr.Sanjay Prabhune,Dr.(Mrs.) Rajshree Somani, and Dr.(Mrs.)V.Nilosy presented research paper on "The Air pollution by Carbon monoxide and its harmful effects". In this paper they focused the air pollution problem with reference to Indore city . On the other hand " Modelling of Air pollution due to vehicular fuel" was presented by Dr. (Mrs.) Leena Paradkar. Prof. S. Bhatt presented a reaserch paper on the modern times burning issue Environmental problems—Nuclear Energy : A source of radioactive pollution. Miss Vandana Mishra presented a research paper on, "Causes of environmental problem : A review of Backward perception." Dr. Alpana Trivedi focused on "Chemical pesticide in Human environment : A serious Health Hazard". Dr. Shobha Sharma presented a research paper on todays alarming problem—"Overdrawing groundwater and its consequences' Miss Shuchi Verma, and Dr. Devendra Kaur jointly presented a research paper related to slums and degradation of environment of Indore city . Mr.Mohan Nimole, Gokul Pal and B.S.Chouhan presented a paper on "Acid rain". Dr. Suvarna Tawase read a paper on the relationship between music and health with environment while Dr. Abha Holker indicated the degradation of ethical environment.

TECHNICAL SESSION—II

Environment, Society and Population

The session started at 3.45 p.m. and concluded at 5.30 p.m. The sub-theme of this session was, "Environment, Society and Population". This session was chaired by Prof. B.C. Vaidya, Pune, co-chaired by Dr. (Mrs.) K.R. Shrivastava Gorakhpur, Prof. S.C. Verma, Indore, was the repporteur in this session. Altogether 18 research papers were presented. Miss. Garima Dongre, Research scholar, presented a paper on the very controversial issue of Dam on river Narmada. Her paper entitled: Indira Sagar Project: Problems of rehabilitation—A Challenge for Environment : A Case Study of HARSUD was a paper of considerable discussion . Dr. Sudha Kapoor presented a research paper on Micro Credit or self-help group in India and also on "Emerging Issues and Challenges in Environmental change", A Reasearch paper entitled Tribal Habitat Environmental Management was presented by Dr. B.L. Patidar and Dr. D.K. Patidar. One of the serious problem of computer age is E-waste Prof. Sumitra Joshi and Prof. Kavita Chandani pointed out the," Electronic waste, A Serious Challenge to the Environment". Mr. Ajay Kumar Rai, Research Scholar, Baba Sahib Ambedkar National Institute Mhow, highlighted environmental pollution and its impact on tribal region. Saishwari Kaul discussed social degradation in Ujjain City. Prof. Neena Baghel pointed out the environment problems in the tribal region of Jhabua District. Dr. Tripti Joshi drew attention on world-wide environmental pollution problem and its effects on human health. Dr.A.S. Mandloi and Dr. S.S. Baghel took the view on Sardar Sarovar Project and its environmental impact.

Cultural Evening

After completion of 1st and 2nd session at 5.30 p.m. the delegates and guests were invited to participate in a cultural programme by college students in the evening which was followed by dinner.

TECHNICAL SESSION—III

Environmental Problems at Local and Regional Level

The session started on 24th Feb. at 9.00 a.m. Prof. B.C. Vaidya, Secretary, DGS., Department of Geography, Pune University, Pune presented a lead paper on "A study of Climatic Conditions of Western Part in Maharashtra State: An Environmental Approach". This study based on Satara district of Maharashtra. It was followed by research paper presentation. In this session 20 research papers were presented. Prof. Y.G.Joshi Dean, Baba Saheb Ambedkar National Institute Mhow, chaired the session. The session was co-chaired by Prof. L.K. Mudgal, Rapporteur was Prof. P. Mone. Dr. Archana Purohit discussed the problems and solutions of disposal of Municipal Waste of Indore city. Dr. Sunita Phadnis and Rekha Killedar analyzed the presence of Pesticides in Water and Associated Health Impacts. An interesting paper, The Problem of Sitting in Office Environment was presented by Prof. Anuradha Awasthi. Problems associated with noise pollution with reference to Indore city were discussed by Dr. Manju Patni and Dr. Sushma Sharma, Lokesh Sharma and Sandeep Sarwan,research scholars analyzed environmental pollution due to religious programmes in Ujjain city. Mrs. Sudha Agrawal and Mrs. Kiran Gupta dealt with "Economic development and environmental degradation with reference to economic region, SEZ."

Mosquito originated diseases are very common in India, the related chapter was analyzed by Rajkumar Nagwanshi and Mrs. Purnima with reference to Indore city. Bagh caves are our historical heritage which is on the verge of degradation due to environment. This critical environmental aspect was discussed by Mrs. Rajshri Vibhute and Mrs. Kavita Paul, Sanjay Chourasia and Sachin Awasthi focused on some environmental issues in Indian context. Sardar Sarovar Project is very controversial issue of river Narmada. An analysis of submergences and rehabilitation problems with reference to Dharmpuri Tahsil was presented by Prof. P.C. Yadav. Watershed mission plays a vital role in conservation of natural resources. It was examined by Prof. Juliet Onkar and Prof. Rekha Verma. The delegates exchanged views during a tea-break which followed the session.

TECHNICAL SESSION—IV

Environmental Concerns and Environmental Impact Assessment

This session started at 11.15 a.m. and was devoted to Environmental concerns and "Environmental Impact Assessment". It was a quite busy session as 25 research papers were presented in the session. This session was chaired by Prof. V.K. Shrivastava, Gorakhpur and rapporteur was Dr. Juliet Onkar, Mhow. It was with lead lecture of Prof. Y.G. Joshi, Dean Bani, Mhow on "Environmental Concern Social Responses and Initiatives" . The lead lecture was followed by research papers of the delegates. Dr. Venu Trivedi presented an experiment-based research paper on the "Quality of Ground Water of Indore City". She examined ground water quality on the basis of 10 selected parameters of different area of the city. Prof. P.Mone took a typical environmental issue, i.e. psychosomatic effect on mind and body, which is abstract environment. Mrs. Bindu Gandhi, Dr. Seema Trivedi and Dr. Sadhana Saxena jointly presented a research paper on a new route to protection on environment, i.e. Green Chemistry. Air quality of Indore was assessed by Dr.D. Kaur and Subra Viswas, Dr. Mrs. Alka Bajpai, highlighted effect of widening of A.B. Road, between two main educational institutes, Govt. Holkar Science College and Govt. Arts and Commerce College, Indore. Dr. V.J. Patil, Dr. S.V.Dhake and Dr. R.V. Bhole assessed the impact of Brick industries on soil resources. Effects of environmental problems were presented by Dr. Deepnita Gargava. Climatic Changes: A Temporal analysis of Indore city was presented by young researcher of M.Phil Geograohy course, Miss. Navita Rajurkar, Miss Manisha Lavanshi, Priyanka Yogi, Mr. Parag Meshram and Ankush Khobargade. Mrs. Sandhya Kothalekar presented a natural method to purify the polluted water. Impact of environmental problems was assessed by Prof. Neeraj Rao and Dr. Anil Kumar Jain. The session was followed by lunch in the college hostel.

TECHNICAL SESSION—V

Environmental Policy, Planning and Management

Technical Session-V contained research papers on "Environmental Policy, Planning and Management". It was started at 2.15 p.m. and concluded at 4.15 p.m. Prof. S.M. Rashid, Jamia Millia Islamia, New Delhi chaired the session and Dr. T.A. Sihorawala, Retd. Prof. Govindram Saksaria Technological Institute, Indore was the chairperson. Dr. Venu Trivedi was the rapporteur in this session. In all 20 research papers were presented in the session. Two lead lectures one of Prof. S.M. Rashid in Environmental problems and policy and the other by Dr. (Mrs.) K.R. Shrivastava, Gorakhpur on floriculture and initiative in sustainable ecology and economy were presented. These lectures were followed by the presentation of research papers. Mrs. Sumita Vyas took a view on solid waste management. Green Revolution, Pros. and Cons. was analyzed by Mrs. Manisha Dandwate. Dr. Gomati Chelani discussed environmental policies and management. Forest reserves of India are degrading very fast. In this context Dr. Rakhee Shukla made an attempt to analyze the perception of people in forest resources. This study was based on forest management. Miss Kanchan Solanki and Prof. Munira Hussain presented a key issue i.e. awareness towards environment.This paper was based on the Malnutrition of children. Nitin Choursia made an attempt to assess the potential of organic farming for soil conservation. Developing a collaborative model for environmental planning and management was revealed by Dr. Rashmi Gupta.and Prof. Vandna Upadhyay. They highlighted the impacts of environmental problems on the society. Mrs. Jyoti Dudhiya and Dr.Anamika Jain analyzed problems and prevention of air pollution. Remote sensing plays a vital role in environmental planning .Prof. Naresh Kumar and Anjula Pois pointed out the application of remote sensing in environmental planning. The highlight of the technical session was the paper on the importance of Organic Farming for the security of environment with reference to Kasturbagram Indore was revealed by a group of young research scholars like Mr. Manoj Sanwale , Mr.Jitendra Thakur , Miss Rani Vaskel, Miss Sandhya Solanki and Miss Arnita Pandare (All M.Phil. students). An effort of the residents of Saket Nagar, Indore city towards solid waste management was depicted by a group of young researchers, Mr. Anilkumar Gohia, Miss Sunita Sahu, Miss Shweta Saryam and Miss Sarita Chouhan.

Valedictory Session

Valedictory session of the National conference started at 4.30 p.m. Presided by Dr. V.K. Shrivastava, Emeritus Fellow, D.D. University, Gorakhpur. The chief guest was Principal

Holkar Science College Dr. N.K. Dhakad and the resource person was Dr. Y.G. Joshi Bani, Mhow. Dr. Manjula Choubey and the convener Dr. Venu Trivedi were also on the dais. The chief guest presented an award for best poster presentation to Miss Garima Dongre a research scholar, Department of Geography, Govt. P.G. Girls College, Motitabela, Indore. Dr. Rakhee Shukla concluded the session. All session reportteurs presented their session's reports. The session also decided to forward the recommendations of the conference to concerned Ministries and departments of Madhya Pradesh Govt., State Planning Commission, societies and organizations working in the field of environment etc.

In the end Dr. Venu Trivedi, the convener of the conference thanked all who contributed towards the success of the conference.

Convener

Index